[handwritten signature]

Nov 13 1984

David Frost's Book of Millionaires, Multimillionaires, and Really Rich People . . . ..

With one
notable
exception!

David

David Frost's Book of Millionaires, Multimillionaires, and Really Rich People

Compiled and
written by
David Frost
and
Michael Deakin

Crown Publishers, Inc.
New York

Library of Congress Cataloging in Publication Data

Frost, David.
    David Frost's Book of millionaires, multimillionaires, and really rich
people.

    1. Millionaires—Anecdotes, facetiae, satire, etc. 2. Millionairesses—
Anecdotes, facetiae, satire, etc. 3. Capitalists and financiers—Anecdotes,
facetiae, satire, etc. 4. Wealth — Anecdotes, facetiae, satire, etc. 5. Mon-
ey—Anecdotes, facetiae, satire, etc. I. Deakin, Michael. II. Title. III. Title:
Book of millionaires, multimillionaires, and really rich people.
HG172.A2F74   1984   305.5'234'0922   84-9498
ISBN 0-517-55444-5

Published by Crown Publishers, Inc., One Park Avenue, New York, New
York 10016

Manufactured in the United States of America

10   9   8   7   6   5   4   3   2   1

First Edition

*C*ontents

Acknowledgments

The compilers would like to thank many friends for their help in the preparation of this book. In particular the names of Professor Nicholas Deakin, Peter Jay and Jim Slater spring to mind. From the noble house of André Deutsch, Diana Athill and the Padrone have once again given their all; and so have Cindy Ballin and Tricia Pombo, in their skilled subliminal management of the lives of Messrs. Deakin and Frost, respectively.

Introduction

When you grow up in a Methodist manse, wealth and the accumulation of wealth are scarcely daily topics at the breakfast table. Indeed, the first real discussion of the subject that I can recall was at school with a teacher telling us all sternly that "a fool and his money are soon parted" and several of us asking how, if that was true, they ever came to get together in the first place. (We were, as you will gather, somewhat naive about death duties and the advantages of having a large inheritance.)

One of the songs on the wireless at the time was "Money is the root of all evil." It was only later that a Sunday school teacher quoted the biblical text from Paul's Letter to Timothy in full: "The love of money is the root of all evil." It was later still that I read in Mark Twain his own variation: "The lack of money is the root of all evil." And it was only during the preparation of this book that I came upon the saying that: "Money is very often the *fruit* of evil, rather than the root of it."

Those four remarks distill several of the often contradictory emotions engendered by the subject of this miscellany. Plato decided the whole business was a no-win proposition. "Wealth is the parent of luxury and indolence," he said, "and poverty of meanness and viciousness"; and as if that wasn't bad enough, he went on to add that discontent was the inevitable child of both.

So who is right about all this? Are millionaires happier and more content than the rest of us? (And when we use the word *millionaire* in this book we usually mean a multimillionaire at least, or better still a budding billionaire.) Or are they perhaps just more restless, more driven?

The first millionaire I ever interviewed was Roy Thomson at the height of his power and wealth in 1966. Did he set out from the beginning with the idea of making money? "Oh always, yes. That was my dominant ambition, and I still want to make it!"

Did he want to make it in any particular way, or just to make it? "Well, I don't run any disorderly houses or anything of that kind, but I mean any legitimate way, yes."

Why, having so much by then, did he still want to make more? "Well, I think it's an obsession you get. You start off on a one-track way, and things keep coming up, and you want to make more money, buy more businesses. And if you want to buy more businesses, you've got to make more money."

"You want to make more money, to buy more businesses?"

"That's right."

"In order to make more money?"

"No doubt of it."

"And when you've got all the businesses you could buy, making all the money . . . what would you have been doing it all *for*?"

"To make more money, to buy more businesses."

For Aristotle Onassis the emphasis lay elsewhere. "It's not a question of money," he said. "After you reach a certain point, money becomes unimportant, what matters is success. The sensible thing would be for me to stop now but I can't. I have to keep aiming higher and higher—just for the thrill." And Jackie Onassis once said of him, "Ari never stops working. He dreams in millions."

Cynics might say that, with his overheads, he had to. But I always had the feeling that his evident enjoyment of Skorpios, the *Christina*, his various homes and the rest was something more than conspicuous consumption gone wild. Fiercely proud of his Mediterranean peasant stock, he had succeeded in creating — and was working to maintain — a private world of his own creation, almost independent of the real one, a world into which he could summon almost anyone he chose from the greatest living Englishman to the most famous and talked-about woman of his time. The fact that toward the end of his life the homelier human values of the real world started to bear in on him more and more and convince him of the emptiness of much of his own creation, was perhaps the ultimate sadness that made the eulogies somehow more tragic than triumphal.

The juxtaposition of the names Thomson and Onassis underlines another basic fact about millionaires — you cannot measure wealth through lifestyle. While Aristotle Onassis was sailing on board the *Christina*, Roy Thomson was economizing on breakfast at a coffee stall on the way to the office.

William Herbert Hunt, the principal manager of the Hunt family's vast oil empire, and probably a billionaire in his own right, was seen during the 1979 energy crisis in his ten-year-old Mercedes waiting patiently with his wife and dog in a two-hour gasoline line. The Richardson-Bass family in Texas, whose fortune is estimated at more than two billion dollars, also live quietly. As one of their friends said to a reporter, "When you're where they are, who do you want to impress?"

This is wealth on the scale of John Paul Getty who once said, "If you know exactly how rich you are, you are not really rich" (against which, gentle reader, remember for your comfort that John Jacob Astor said: "A man who has a million dollars is as well off as if he were rich").

But when you have made it, there comes the multiple-choice question of what to do with it. Another Texas oil man, Clint Murchison Sr., passed on to his sons several hundred million each, and the simple advice, "Money is a lot like manure. Pile it in one place and it stinks like hell. Spread it around, and it does a lot of good."

Andrew Carnegie went further, believing that the super-rich could really play a benign and central role in the affairs of their fellow citizens: "Thus is the problem of the rich and the poor to be solved. Individualism will continue, but the millionaire will be but a trustee of the poor, entrusted for a season with a great part of the increased wealth of the community, but administering it for the common good far better than it could or would have done for itself."

I doubt very much whether the readers of this book will feel that Carnegie's utopian dream has often become a reality, but he underlined his own sincerity by saying on one occasion, "The man who dies rich, dies disgraced."

Whether it is dealing with Andrew Carnegie, William Beckford, or indeed Croesus, much of this book is of course historical. But when we talked to people about who, in their opinion, was a modern day reincarnation of some of the larger-than-life figures in this book, the name that recurred most frequently was that of Sir James Goldsmith. He is extrovert, they said, and controversial, and he has made it big. When I spoke to him, however, he rather surprisingly said that he doubted whether he qualified for inclusion. Then he explained why. "I am not entirely sure that I have succeeded in the way you mean. I also feel that any businessman who thinks he has succeeded before he has left the table and cashed his chips has not yet succeeded and is in great danger of losing everything if he gets confident. Every gambler knows he's not winning until he's cashed his chips and left the table. Being ahead means nothing. It's being ahead at the end of the game.

"Some people go on because the actual process of making it has become more important than the actual product. Some because they are frightened of being bored. And this is their whole life. Some go on because they are very narrow people. You don't have to be a broad or intelligent person to succeed in business. Probably the opposite. Probably the right kind of mind is the narrow, laser-beamed and orderly mind suitably buffered by greed and fear, and then of course, luck. But probably that sort of person would be terrified of retiring, because he wouldn't know what to do once retired. There is no other life to go to. So they never get off the treadmill. Because it's only the treadmill that they enjoy."

Did he think that it would have been more fun to have been rich two or three centuries ago, before twentieth century taxation, and twentieth century envy, seem to have almost driven many millionaires underground?

"I don't think it is a question of envy and tax, though both of them have influence. I think it's a question of culture. There have been certain times in history when the whole culture of a particular civilization has been especially welcoming to a way of life you can enjoy when you've got money. A particular example is Paris between 1890 and 1910, or Paris before Sedan, under Napoleon III. That was a time when the French culture and way of life was probably at its most agreeable. Where the social mobility was sufficient to allow a rich man to get in and spend his money, whereas before that the social mobility was probably too restricted. Even after the last war, places like Cannes and Deauville were incredibly luxurious and glamorous. Where everyone you saw, you had heard of. Which I could only watch from the outside but I watched it with fascination. Someone who's got money today can't go back to that sort of life, because that sort of life has disappeared. It's the culture."

Which part of his business career had given him the most pleasure? Was it the first time he made money, or when he made more? "Oh, the first time. I'd sold a third of my business and as I drove home I sang all the way as I realized for the first time in my life I wasn't poor."

In general, did he think that millionaires are happier than everyone else? "I think it has to depend on the individual. Money can't buy happiness. But then again, happiness can't buy money! It's very complicated. I have seen people who have been made positively unhappy by making money. There is a very old Chinese proverb that those that the gods hate, they satisfy their ambitions. That can happen. But in general I think I would have to agree with Woody Allen: money is better than poverty—if only for financial reasons."

Readers will reach their own conclusions about which of the millionaires in this book were being punished by the gods, and which were being rewarded; about whether they were desperately trying to fill an aching void, or fulfilling their wildest dreams, or using money, or being used by it.

However, since the millionaires' money in this book is, to quote Mark Twain, twice tainted—"'tain't yours and 'tain't mine"—perhaps during some of the more bizarre exploits recounted we should in all fairness bear in mind the cautionary words of L. P. Smith: "To suppose, as we all suppose, that we could be rich and not behave the way the rich behave, is like supposing that we could drink all day and stay sober."

Nevertheless, there will, I suspect, be times in the course of the foibles that follow when even such a modest and measured defense will prove somewhat difficult to endorse.

David Frost's Book of Millionaires, Multimillionaires, and Really Rich People

Pushing Out
the Boat...

Second only to palaces, castles, follies and such, your average millionaire likes yachts. Perhaps the fashion was set by Cleopatra — certainly one of the first big spenders — who around 1 B.C. used to take her boyfriends for day trips on the Nile in a barge with a poop of beaten gold, and purple sails drenched in so much scent that the wind itself seemed perfumed. The oars were silver and the lady reclined in a cloth-of-gold tent while the ship's orchestra played melting music. For a good many centuries only kings or emperors could afford to follow an example so extravagant, but in modern times commoners started to compete — their motto apparently being the bigger the better.

Commodore Cornelius Vanderbilt nearly spoiled the whole thing for succeeding generations of millionaires by setting an unbeatable record right at the start. Having reached the age of fifty-nine without ever taking a holiday, he decided that the time for a little relaxation had come so he might as well take it in comfort. Accordingly, he ordered a yacht to be built the size of an ocean liner: the twenty-five hundred ton *North Star*. At her launching in 1853 she was said to have cost half a million dollars.

Interior decoration and furnishings accounted for a fair bit of this stupendous sum. The main saloon was paneled throughout in rosewood — genuine Louis XV, so it was said. The family's quarters consisted of ten state-rooms

1

enameled in white, with lace hangings. Other saloons were decorated respectively in green and gold, scarlet and gold, and orange and gold, and a balmy temperature was maintained by "Van Horn's patent steam heaters," concealed behind elaborate bronze screens. Other parts of the yacht were encrusted with granite from Naples, yellow marble from the Pyrenees and jasper from Brescia. Not surprisingly, the *North Star* became a talking point throughout America. As one local newspaper put it, with modest pride: "What will the wealthy noblemen of England—all proprietors of sailing yachts of fifty and a hundred tons—say to a citizen of the United States appearing in their waters with a steamship yacht of twenty-five hundred tons burthen: a vessel large enough to carry the armaments of the British seventy-four!"

The gratifying answer to that question was that the British were stunned, and compared Commodore Vanderbilt—much to his delight—to Cosimo de Medici.

Even the crew of the *North Star* was extraordinary, including as it did many young men of good family who had signed on simply to be near the Commodore, in the hope that his eye might light on them and that some smidgin of his amazing gift for money-making might rub off on them. There was also a ship's doctor, all the necessary officers and a sky-pilot, the Rev. John Overton Coules ("The Commodore does the swearing; I do the praying"). By the time Vanderbilt's holiday cruise was over—it had included a progress round both the Mediterranean and the Baltic, as well as calling in on Britain and Russia—it was said that his yacht had "been admired by the Russian court, gazed at by the Sultan, astonished John Bull and frightened the Pope."

What millionaire could have asked for more?

Succeeding generations of the super-rich, determined to carry on the tradition, hit on a brilliant way of competing with Vanderbilt's splendor without being made to feel small. When the banker J. P. Morgan was showing someone around his yacht, his guest asked what it cost to run such a leviathan. J. P. smiled condescendingly and replied: "Nobody who has to ask what a yacht costs has any business owning one." Since when, not bothering to ask what your yacht cost has pretty obviously been the technique of pleasure-boat owners from Agnelli and Khashoggi to Niarchos and Onassis.

Most famous of these yachts, of course, was Onassis's *Christina*, named for his daughter. This yacht had begun life in more military fashion as a Canadian navy frigate. The Greek shipping tycoon, however, had it remodeled at a cost in 1954 of three million dollars ($10.4 million today). For this he got the usual gold taps in the Siena marble bathrooms. Rather more exotic were barstools covered with whales' testicles — and rather more precious to the future comfort of mankind, not one but two El Grecos. Even the clothes on the dolls in the nursery were by Dior — and the whole thing cost upwards of a million and a half dollars a year to run. Commodore Vanderbilt would have felt at home.

At the start of this century there was a smattering of millionaires who couldn't be bothered with yachts and were content to slum their way across the Atlantic on a Cunarder or a ship of the French Line. Life on one of the blue ribbon runs, they argued, was not unbearably austere. For example, if you were a run-of-the-mill, small-town millionaire who had booked a passage on the Cunard Line's *Aquitania*, under Commodore Sir James Charles, your dinner at the Commodore's table would have gone like this: "Stewards wheeled in carcasses of whole roast oxen one night, and the next evening small herds of grilled antelopes surrounded a hilltop of Strasbourg pâté de foie gras surmounted with peacock fans. Electrically illuminated *pièces montées* representing the battle of Waterloo and other patriotic moments made an appearance while the ship's orchestra played Elgar. Chefs in two-foot-high hats emerged

3

to make thrusts at turrets of Black Angus, and souffles the size of the same chefs' hats blossomed over a Paine's firework display of the Fourth of July. All the while champagne circulated in jeroboams: Mumm 1916, Irroy and Perrier Jouet ditto."

The passengers disembarked at Cherbourg or New York, somewhat more portly, no doubt, but otherwise none the worse for the crossing. It was the Commodore himself who paid the price. It was while he was attacking a pastry castle surrounded by a moat of diamond-back turtle stew à la Madeira that he keeled over and slipped his moorings for ever. When they took his corpse ashore at Southampton they had to open both wings of the *Aquitania*'s half ports in order to accommodate his passing.

One passenger on the *Aquitania* who would not have sat at the captain's table was Tom Mix's Wonder Horse, Tony (an example like Incitatus, the nag raised to the Senate by Caligula, of that rare species the equine millionaire). He and Tom made the crossing comfortably, taking daily exercise round the deck.

As did H. E. and Arabella Huntington, probably the richest of the fabulous California millionaires. It was a special feature of the *Aquitania* that every state-room or suite was decorated with reproductions of great paintings. On one crossing the Huntingtons were in the Gainsborough suite, and Arabella fell in love with "The Blue Boy". Her husband must buy her the original, she said, so her husband asked Lord Duveen to act for him. The painting belonged to the Duke of Westminster, who had never thought of selling it and was astonished at being offered six hundred thousand dollars for it out of the blue, as it were. In spite of his surprise he did the decent thing, and accepted. The only trouble was that when it arrived in California the Huntingtons didn't like it very much. They said that it was a lot greener than the reproduction that had so delighted them in their cabin.

4

Not everyone's Atlantic crossing was so pleasant. John Jacob Astor—one of the world's richest men at the time, known as "the world's greatest monument to unearned increment"—was a passenger on the *Titanic*, with sundry other millionaires, on that ill-fated maiden voyage. When the iceberg was hit and it turned out that the ship, although long on jeroboams of Taittinger, was short on lifeboats, the gallant Astor gave up his chance of safety and went down with the ship. His body was eventually found "dressed in a blue suit, standing almost erect in a lifebelt"—with twenty-five hundred dollars still in his pocket.

Astor was not the only member of the super-rich to face eternal equality as a result of the *Titanic*'s sinking. The sum he couldn't take with him was reputed to top a hundred and fifty million dollars ($888 million today). His fellow victim Benjamin Guggenheim weighed in at—or out of—ninety-five millions ($562 million today) and two other passengers, Messrs. Wider and Strauss, left behind fifty millions each ($296 millions today). Bruce Ismay, the man who owned the stricken ship, shuffled off his mortal coil and a mere forty million dollars ($237 million today). Only the Vanderbilts remained lucky in their dealings with things nautical. Alfred Gwynne Vanderbilt, the Commodore's son, had intended to sail on the *Titanic* for its maiden voyage, but changed his mind at the last moment.

*C*onspicuous Consumption

The nineteenth century Rothschild family kept great state in, among other places, their home at Waddesdon, where Alfred Rothschild lived. One day Prime Minister Asquith, who was staying from Friday till Monday, was waited on at teatime by the butler. The following conversation ensued:

"Tea, coffee or a peach from off the wall, sir?"

"Tea, please."

"China, Indian or Ceylon, sir?"

"China, please."

"Lemon, milk or cream, sir?"

"Milk, please."

"Jersey, Hereford or Shorthorn, sir? . . ."

Meanwhile, in America, Alice Vanderbilt, wife of Cornelius Vanderbilt II, had the water taps in her brass and marble bathroom in her country home, "Breakers," labeled, "Hot," "Cold" and "Salt."

Diamonds Are a Girl's Best Friend

Millionaires have often said it with rocks, as lesser mortals say it with flowers, and wise girls have always accepted them.

Gordon Selfridge, the store tycoon, took the banality out of such a gift by choosing an original setting. When he gave the notorious Dolly Sisters a pair of fine four-carat blue diamonds, he got the house of Cartier—always willing to oblige in a good cause—to set the stones in the shells of a well-matched pair of tortoises. The Sisters used to take the creatures for walks on the front at Le Touquet, to the particular delight of crustacea fanciers among the onlookers.

The actress Lillian Russell attracted similar crowds whenever she took a spin on her bicycle, given her by the ever-generous Diamond Jim Brady. This unusually elegant velocipede had handlebars inlaid with mother-of-pearl, while the spokes of its wheels must have twinkled and flashed in a most eye-catching way, considering that they were encrusted with diamonds, sapphires, rubies and emeralds. When on tour and covering distances too great for pedaling, so that she had to travel by train, the prudent comedienne would keep her bicycle safe on the journey in a specially designed traveling case made of the finest Moroccan leather.

8

From time to time Miss Russell, when she dismounted in order to tread the stage, may well have been scrutinized through a pair of mother-of-pearl and diamond opera glasses. They were given by Congressman John Morrissey to his wife for Christmas 1860. He had them made for him in Paris, at a cost of ten thousand dollars. But then, conspicuous consumption was the order of the day. When Ned McLean, owner of the *Washington Post*, presented his wife with the Hope Diamond by way of a sweetener, she threw a party costing forty thousand dollars ($207,792 today) just to welcome it — what, after all, would be the point of owning a spectacular rock if none of your friends knew you had it?

Perhaps the oddest way of deploying diamonds was that thought up by one Ned Green, who collected chamber pots and chastity belts that had been studded with them. Let us

9

hope he kept them in cabinets rather than giving them to his lady friends, who might well have found such gifts somewhat double-edged.

The trouble with sparklers is that they look so desirable to so many people in addition to their owners: security is always a problem. Mrs. Cartwright Wetherill of Philadelphia, for example, had a collection of jewelry so valuable (the most trivial thing in it was an emerald of twenty carats) that a bank vault alone was not considered adequate protection. Accordingly, in addition to keeping it in such a vault, she had it insured — all risks — by Lloyds of London, who would only accept the responsibility on condition that every time she wanted to take some bauble out, she obtained their permission. Since Lloyds and Mrs. Wetherill were three thousand miles apart, this had to be done by telegram — a tedious business that took a touch of glitter out of the lady's more spontaneous party going.

However, it is perhaps better to be overcautious than careless. Consider the case of Helena Rubinstein who, when crossing the Channel in 1956, lightly tossed an empty tissue box over the ship's rail. Perhaps the good lady was suffering from mal-de-mer and was thus less alert than usual, for she overlooked the fact that while improving (if that were possible) her exquisite maquillage in the privacy of her cabin she had taken off a pair of double-diamond earrings and put them into that box. Seventy-thousand dollars worth ($244,389 today) of diamonds, uninsured, disappeared under the choppy grey waves.

As Mrs. Rubinstein tottered ashore, she must have wished that her diamonds had been less authentic, like a notorious tiepin once flaunted by Barney Barnato, the cockney "card" who sold the Kimberley tip to Cecil Rhodes for a bucket of the sparklers. After he had retired to Park Lane, this man with a heart of pure diamond became a famous giver of gifts and a well-known wag. Once, when he was bidden out on the town by some friends, the invitation arrived too late for him to go home and dress, so on his way to dinner Mr. Barnato popped into an outfitter on the Charing Cross Road and bought a pair of paste studs and a paste tiepin of splendiferous vulgarity. Over dinner, as the champagne flowed and the Whitstable oysters slipped smoothly down the throats of one and all, the Diamond King's fellow roisterers were unable to take their eyes off the beacon of light glittering on his shirt front.

"By Jove, that's a cracker—good old Kimberley!" one of them finally exclaimed.

Barnato waved his Romeo y Julieta expansively. "Anyone who wants it—all he has to do is pay for the wine tonight," he said.

They almost knocked the wine steward over in their rush to pick up the tab; and only when copious Krug for six had been duly paid for did Barnato reveal that the tiepin, together with the studs, had cost him ninepence.

*G*etting the Builders In

What most of us want ardently after getting the builders in, is to get them out again, but the Philadelphia matron Mrs. Eva Stotesbury had greater stamina than that.

She was accustomed to thinking big — in 1915 her husband Ned had an income of over seven million dollars a year, and she set about spending it. Whitemarsh Hall, the first house she had run up, was six stories tall and had a hundred and forty-seven rooms, which included forty-five bedrooms, a tailor's shop, a barber's shop and quarters for a resident couturier and a hairdresser. Each guest was allotted a personal chauffeur, and there were seventy gardeners to tend and trim the three hundred acres of formal garden.

In 1925, feeling in need of R and R, the Stotesburys decided to buy a cozy little holiday retreat at Mount Desert Island, Maine, from the president of the Pennsylvania Railroad. The only thing wrong with it was its size, or rather its lack of size. "It has only fifteen servants' rooms," explained Mrs. Stotesbury, "and we shall need at least forty." So she instructed her architect to have the place pulled down and to build a new one that must be ready by next season.

Bricklayers laid bricks, stonemasons dressed masonry, tilers tiled, plumbers plumbed, painters painted and carpenters carpented night and day. When Mrs. Stotesbury returned for the summer of 1926 she found the "cottage" rebuilt from the ground up, and ready for her to move in, although it still smelled pretty strongly of fresh paint. She toured it with her architect.

"How do you like it, Mrs. Stotesbury," he finally asked, pink with not unreasonable pride in his achievement.

"It won't do," she answered. "It's still far too small. It must come down and be built again — and this time I shall stay here to see that it is done properly."

Another rich American woman was quite satisfied with a house that she had bought, but objected to its location. She therefore had the house moved on rollers — an appallingly difficult process that took several weeks, during which her long-suffering husband popped in to the back door every evening and went to his dressing-room to change for dinner.

But the prize for residential mobility must go to a Belgian Baron, Edouard Empain. He was a builder of railways and tramways, and at the turn of the century equipped Cairo with its transport system and its electricity grid; after which he turned to development and ran up a whole city on the outskirts of Cairo, named Heliopolis. He then decided that he wanted a house there for himself that would always face the sun, whatever the time of day, so he designed a Gothic-style pile in red brick, of a kind then fashionable in Flanders, adorned it with statues of naked youths, and set it on a turntable modeled on those used to turn round trams at the end of their lines. The Egyptians took the naked youths in their stride, but were fascinated by the house's constant motion — indeed, it was a talking point far beyond Cairo. It still stands, although time and sand have, alas, done in the complex gyrations of the turntable, and indeed of the good baron himself.

Money to Burn

The super-rich are often said to have "money to burn." Few have actually ever done so. The glorious exception to this rule was billionaire James Gordon-Bennett, a notable eccentric who at the beginning of the century named his yacht the *Lysistrata*, "after" — as he said — "a Greek lady who was reported to have been very beautiful and very fast."

Apart from his yacht, Mr. Gordon-Bennett seemed to have only one passion — to get through all the money of which he was possessed. He did well, since in all he managed to dispose of forty million dollars ($280 million today). On one occasion, sensing the pace slackening, he gave a tip of fourteen thousand dollars ($98,000 today) to the guard on the Train Bleu between Paris and Monte Carlo. The fellow stepped off the train, resigned from the employment of the Grand Compagnie des Wagons Lits and opened a restaurant.

Another example of Gordon-Bennett's eccentric but ultimately rewarding attitude toward good service was evoked by his love of a good Southdown mutton chop, grilled to a delicate pink. To his great pleasure he found a restaurant in Monte Carlo which could cook such chops to a turn. Night after night he would go there to take his supper — until one evening he found to his horror that someone else was occupying his favorite table. He summoned the owner — and ordered him then and there to sell him the restaurant. The startled patron at first refused, but on being told that money was no object, sold out on the

spot for $40,000 ($280,000 today). Having become the pro-
prietor of all he surveyed, the millionaire asked the offending party to vacate his favorite table and leave at once,
even though they were only halfway through their meal.

After seating himself comfortably at his table and enjoy-
ing his Southdown chops without further interruption,
Gordon-Bennett proceeded to give the restaurant to the
waiter by way of a tip. As he left, he asked the new pro-
prietor his name: "Ciro, sir," the grateful fellow replied —
and the restaurant that then took his name became world
famous.

When not satisfying his appetite for lamb chops,
Gordon-Bennett was the publisher of the *New York Herald*
and other organs. After some years he decided to move his
enterprises to Herald Square, between Sixth Avenue and
Broadway. To stand on the top of the new skyscraper the
millionaire ordered a pair of gilt statues, soon known affec-
tionately to the populace of New York as Ike and Mike. The
cost $200,000 ($1,244,000 today).

Naturally the tower included an office for the boss — but Bennett was too busy actually to visit his office. He was mostly off sailing and indulging in his favorite food. However, one day when passing through Tiffany's he saw a new desk set, encrusted with silver in the arabesque style. He remembered his new office and ordered that it be installed forthwith. The cost: $14,000 ($98,000 today).

Four years passed and his new headquarters building became one of the sights of New York. Reluctantly, the millionaire decided that he too had better visit his building, and maybe even take a look at his own office. Accordingly, he brought his yacht into New York harbor and took a taxi into Manhattan. On the way he stopped to take his luncheon at the Union Club. According to his custom, he chose mutton chops — but alas, they were horribly overdone. So great was Gordon-Bennett's displeasure that, after threatening the entire staff with dismissal and the chef with worse, he stormed out of his club and back to his yacht, to set sail without another thought for his new office. As it happened, he never returned.

But the exploit that earns Gordon-Bennett a chapter of his own, and which is still recalled in song and fable, took place when he was interviewing a young man for a job on another of his papers, the *Paris Herald.* Suddenly he began to wriggle and writhe about in his chair as though in agony, so that his would-be employee wondered whether the great man was having a seizure. Then, with an oath, Gordon-Bennett tugged a large bundle of thousand-franc notes from his back pocket, where they had been causing discomfort to his posterior, and flung them into the fire. The horror-struck young journalist, thinking that surely he couldn't mean them to burn, sprang from his chair and snatched them from the flames before they were more than scorched. "Give them to me!" the millionaire thundered, purple with indignation. "That's where I *want* them to be." And he threw them back into the blaze.

A Millionaire's Best Friend

Considering how beastly some of the millionaires turned up by our researches seem to have been, it is hardly surprising to learn that there have been rich people who took to sharing their lives, and their millions, with animals.

In the nineteenth century they still more or less limited themselves to dogs. The Duchess of York for example, during the 1850s, kept no fewer than forty hounds around the house, whose various smells caused her guests considerable distress. It was assumed, naturally enough, that she was crazy about dogs — or "the curs," as she called them. The truth was, however, that she tended to blow hot and cold about them. When given a new dog, as often as not she would dose it only too conclusively with opium, and the "best friends" reposing under the sixty-four marble-topped tombs in the grounds of the royal house had not all met with entirely natural deaths.

The vastly rich Earl of Bridgewater, with an annual income of £40,000, was kinder than the Duchess toward his pets, even though they took second place in his passions. First place he reserved for boots, of which he owned three hundred and sixty-five pairs, one for each day of the year. His dogs had to make do with a mere dozen pairs each, matching the Earl's in color and texture, in which to take the air with their master in the Bois de Boulogne. But although he was less generous to them than he might have been in the matter of footwear, he did often allow them to

18

dine at his table. Sometimes they would be dressed for the occasion in the yellow Bridgewater livery, sometimes in hunting pink. The Earl seldom attracted human guests....

And there was certainly one occasion in the career of Mrs. Stuyvesant Fish of Newport, Long Island, when she didn't either. The meal served that day was a feast of liver and rice, followed by a fricassee of bones and pâté de foie gras, and her cohosts were Harry Lehr and a monkey, whose name is not recorded. The guests: one hundred Newport lapdogs.

Pâté de foie gras for pooches may seem extravagant, but it is nothing to the tokens of love bordering on respect that HH the Maharajah of Baroda used to lavish on his favorite elephants. Outdoing the Emperor Haile Selassie, who had diamond collars made for his chihuahua, Baroda gave each of his tuskers a gold chain costing £25,000 (£554,511 today) to wear for the Hindu equivalent of Sunday best.

The Rothschilds were special in their pets, as in every-thing. No ordinary dogs, no dull ruminative cows, for them. They went for performing animals, and Friday to Monday guests at Halton, one of the country houses of Alfred, Lord Rothschild, would be treated to a full-scale performance by trained dogs, ponies, hens and cocks. Lord Rothschild himself, complete with top hat and lavender gloves, would crack the ringmaster's whip.

No doubt the elephants enjoyed parading in their gran-deur, but the tame seal of millionaire Ned McLean was perversely unable to appreciate its luck. Mr. McLean was determined that it should be his drinking companion, but the seal, more accustomed to water than to large quanti-ties of Tennessee sippin' whiskey, expired.

Jay Gould's cow, on the other hand, lived to a ripe old age, in spite of leading a life which, for a cow, was unusu-ally *mouvementé*. Not wishing to be deprived of his bovine friend's company, nor of her product, Mr. Gould had a spe-cial cow car attached to the rear of his private train.

Family customs die hard, and Charles Rothschild, too, liked unusual animals. In his case it was fleas, an interest carried on today by his relative Miriam. In 1908 Charles published a learned paper on the parasites, and on his death he left his entire collection, annotated and cata-logued, to the Science Museum.

The last wills and testaments of many rich people have taken account of their animals, though usually they give something to the animal, rather than giving it away. Argu-ably the richest dog in the world is Viking, a German shepherd who inherited an entire block of real estate in Munich in 1971 (it will go to various animal charities when he dies). Runners-up are the canine chums Mac and George. Their owner, a Californian prune farmer named Thomas Shewbridge, left his entire estate, valued at $112,000 ($248,888 today) to be invested for his dogs, who regularly attend meetings of shareholders and directors.

A tomcat named Buster had his inheritance of $100,000 cut down to a mere $40,000 because the other heirs of his master, Woodbury Rand, challenged the will and won their case. Another will that was challenged was that of Edward Chester of Queensland, Australia, whose six nephews, together with his sister, took grave exception to his leaving £42,000 (£144,574 today) to his racing pigeons.

Richest of all the animal beneficiaries must be the much-loved sheep, Clwyd, who inherited £301,416 from his adopted father, John Leeming. Mr. Leeming had already written a biography of his sheep-son, entitled *One of the Family*, before seeing that he should want for nothing for the rest of his natural life. The fact that Clwyd used to follow his master wherever he went of course contained no element of calculation. . . .

Hitherto we have been considering rich people who loved — or exploited — animals as pets, but when the redoubtable Mrs. Eva Stotesbury exclaimed "I just *adore* alligator," she meant something rather different. The form in which she adored it was that of the hatbox and traveling case. When it occurred to her that she was lacking the complete matching set of luggage without which any American matron of good standing would naturally feel deprived, she must have thought of going shopping to Louis Vuitton; but either she had become bored with shopping, or she didn't quite trust Vuitton to supply her with cases that matched perfectly. So she resolved to take matters — and a gun — into her own hands, and off she went on safari. She soon bagged enough alligators for a set of luggage exactly to her taste — which cost her half a million dollars.

An Idea Whose Time Has Come

One way to immense wealth is often said to be having the right idea at the right time. Consider, for example, the good timing of two men who happened to sit down and put on their thinking caps in 1888, just before the dawn of the new century. One was George Eastman of Rochester, New York, who had the inspiration to invent a camera in the shape of a little portable box, which could be taken anywhere, and whose marketing — with the slogan "You push the button — we do the rest" — was as clever as his invention.

Meanwhile across the Atlantic in Belfast, a veterinary surgeon named Dunlop got tired of hearing his son complain that his bicycle ride to school was too bumpy. Doctor Dunlop turned his mind to the problem, and soon young Dunlop was skimming his way to school on rubber filled with air — for which he was not in the least grateful because his classmates teased him silly about what they called his "pudding tires." The good Doctor, however, once he had marketed this simple brainwave, became exceedingly rich.

He also immortalized himself for posterity by giving his name to a whole range of consumer durables. A select company of millionaires share the same distinction — from Clarence Birdseye who in 1924 developed the idea of frozen food — and sold out to the Postum Company within five years for twenty-two million dollars ($120 million today) — to Laszlo Biro who in 1919 invented the ball pen which in Europe is known by his name.

Today's white-hot ideas tend to be technical to the point of obscurity, and to have their being in Silicon Gulch where all the computer wizards have set up (the place is chip-deep in millionaires who have managed to "tame the frame" and so on). But the public can still single out the name chosen by two such wizards for their product: Apple. Apple? you might say. What an odd name for the first home computer! Its origins say something about its gentle inventors. Their names were Steven Jobs, aged twenty-one, and Stephen Wozniak, aged a venerable twenty-six. They were friends from high school, a pair of long-haired vegetarians who constantly munched apples as they bent over their printed circuit boards. When the idea for a computer for the home came to them, they tried to interest their respective employers in it and were turned down flat — even by firms as astute as Atari and Hewlett-Packard.

On receiving no encouragement, Steven and Stephen went to work on their idea in a family garage in Cupertino, California. From this garage, in their first year, they sold two million dollars' worth of computers. Two years later, having moved to more commodious premises, they sold seventy-five millions worth.

One millionaire, whose wealth is part of folklore but whose name is almost totally unknown, is "the man who invented cat's-eyes." For generations bickering children have been stilled by their fathers on long car journeys by the thought of how much the man who invented those cat's-eyes must have made, even at a halfpenny each. Well, such a man did exist. His name was Percy Shaw, and as a good Yorkshireman he spent his wealth, not on ostentation, but on the things that really matter. Thus until quite recently he would repair every night to his local pub — albeit by Rolls-Royce — and there surround himself with sufficient Tadcaster ales for the evening and a cardboard box full of potato chips. In front of him in the Snug Bar stood four television sets: one, he would explain to his fellow revelers, for BBC1, one for BBC2, one for ITV and one for color.

Guess Who Is Coming to Dinner

William Beckford was the richest man in Europe. His father, Alderman Beckford, had cornered the market in sugar and owned much of Jamaica, which made him the late-eighteenth-century equivalent of an oil sheikh. William was also, insofar as his overpowering wealth allowed, a man of talent and sensibility. He was taught music by Mozart and painting by Fuseli, and wrote a celebrated (though nowadays a mite impenetrable) Gothic novel named *Vathek*.

He also built an even more celebrated house at Fonthill in Wiltshire, where he had been born. In 1800 he had the old house pulled down and his new Fonthill Abbey—a vast Gothic fantasy—erected. Its chief glory was a tower that soared two hundred feet, and the speed with which it was designed and executed was staggering—only too literally so, as it transpired.

The reason for the mad haste was that Beckford had invited Lord Nelson, in company with Emma Hamilton and her *mari complaisant*, Sir William, to dine with him—and to his absolute amazement they had accepted. Beckford had good reason to be astonished since he was an outcast in society even with his vast wealth, owing to his rather unorthodox sexual habits. But then Nelson himself wasn't the acme of sexual respectability—and enjoyed flattery and a good dinner in almost equal proportions. Unfortunately, in the hurry to get things ready for the historic dinner, Beckford's builders simply left out the foundations.

The vast Gothic tower did manage to stay up for the next twenty-five years. Indeed, even when it fell down the tower still had its part to play, knocking down the rest of the extraordinary palace Beckford had built for the fashionable guests who had so rigorously declined to follow Nelson's example.

The same wish to entertain an important guest in a suitable manner caused an American gentleman named Tom Walsh and his wife, the lovely Evelyn, to include a throne room on the third floor of their house at 2020 Massachusetts Avenue in Washington. It was equipped with a hydraulic lift, so that at the touch of a button a gilt and velvet throne would rise out of the floor. This cost $5,075 ($26,363 today) but seemed to the Walshes cheap at the price, since their good friend the king of the Belgians might drop in at any moment.

Unfortunately, their meeting with the king had been only fleeting and had made less impression on His Majesty than it did on them. In this case the foundations stood firm— but the guest never materialized.

Lord Kitchener, as befitted a distinguished soldier, took a splendidly millionairish attitude toward a problem he encountered connected with entertainment. Once, while in Calcutta he was informed that there was simply no room to accommodate the fifteen hundred guests that Lord Hamilton had asked to a reception in his honor. The general, therefore, promptly set about creating a pleasantly verdant ambience fit for such a reception. Eight hundred coolies were summoned and ordered to fill in a ditch, rake up the stones and bring whole cartloads of plants and shrubs down from the nearest hill station. They were then ordered to sprinkle the whole area with sand, water it well, and— under the stern eye of the general—sow every inch of it with mustard and cress.

Thirty-six hours later the guests stood marveling at the display of flowers and shrubs, and even more at the smooth stretches of emerald-green lawns. Nothing like them had ever before been seen in India. Verily, they said, Lord Kitchener could make the desert bloom.

A Hint of Eastern Promise

When education and the advent of air travel just before the last war finally put an end to the Hindu belief that a man would lose his soul by crossing the black waters, the princes of the Indian Empire flocked to Europe. Once here, they holed up in the Savoy and the Dorchester, in the Ritz and the Negresco, and spent, and spent, and spent. Nothing seemed too much for them.

For instance, the Maharanee of Cooch Behar, known as "Ma," was renowned as a hostess so particular as to her guests' comfort that she would inspect each guest chamber in her palace, even going so far as to lie on their beds to make sure that their reading lights were properly adjusted. The same princess, in the 1930s, upon hearing that the best pasta was to be had only in a certain small bistro in Rome, sent her cook all the way from India to study there. When the poor fellow protested that his Muslim soul would be in jeopardy in a country awash with wine, aperitifs and liqueurs, she insisted that her retainer take to drink as well. "It is not alcohol," she told him, "but an essential part of the food that my guests must have prepared for them." Thus absolved by his sovereign princess from mortal sin, the cook got good and drunk every night.

Rich and strong-willed the Maharanee of Cooch Behar may have been—but her extravagances abroad were as nothing compared with the life-style enjoyed by the Cooch Behars at home. Their palace—no doubt so as to show

how very modern and patriotically minded they were —
had been built to the same design as the Victoria and Albert
Museum in London. Inside, a roller skating rink, in the style
of Alexandra Palace, provided distraction for some thirty
junior members of the princely family. A thirty-five-piece
orchestra, substantially outnumbering the skaters, provided a lilting accompaniment of waltzes to add to the
general excitement. Music also played a part at the family
table where dinners, complete with such proper European
delicacies as Brown Windsor Soup and Bread-and-Butter
Pudding, were consumed to the sound of *The Mikado*
played by a military band. French champagne was used to
wash the whole lot down.

Next to European food, and Indian dancing girls, your

average maharajah liked motor cars above all else. They were imported from Europe by the boatload. Soon the dusty roads of princely India thrummed and purred with the coming and going of rosewood-paneled, boat-tailed Lanchesters, gold-plated Isotto-Fraschinis and silver Hispanos, as well as of Rolls-Royces designed for shooting tigers, or transporting Muslim princesses in purdah. (One prince, Jaipur, even took to flying, and imported a series of spindly biplanes.) The skeletons of princely vehicles still litter the garages of the palaces of India, tireless, without batteries, but lovingly tended by their faithful grooms.

As if this were not enough, one maharajah combined the twin passions for European food and transportation and duly had a silver train set crafted by the reliable Bassett Lowke company to run on rails around the dinner table at his palace bearing salt, pepper and mustard, while all the time alluringly emitting puffs of smoke. Alas, upon the very first occasion that it was used it went terribly wrong, tore wildly around the table and spilled its freight of condiments into the laps of the royal guests. After which it went on static display.

Not all the habits of the maharajahs were as endearing. One of them, the Maharajah of Patiala, took to executing his polo ponies after they had failed him during a chukka, by gunning them down on the spot with his Webley and Scott pistol. The British who had turned something of a blind eye to his rather esoteric activities with selected cadets from his private army—goings-on that, as in the case of the polo ponies, sometimes led to deaths as well as to fates worse than—decided that he must be deposed.

Another of them, the Gaekwar of Baroda, tried to poison the British resident, Sir Robert Phayre, who telegraphed, stiff upper-lipped, to his head office in Poona: "Bold attempt to poison me today has been providentially frustrated. More by next post."

The offending prince was duly deposed.

The two richest of the princely maharajahs, however, lived blameless if hardly retiring lives. The new-style, reformed Prince of Baroda, for instance, owned a patch the size of Yorkshire and Lincolnshire combined. Like all of his fellow princes he was obsessed by the number of guns in his salute. The cunning British had more or less succeeded in ruling the whole of princely India by means of adding or subtracting a gun here or a gun there in the ration of ceremonial cannon shots a princely house could claim as its due. Baroda, however, short-circuited the whole thing by having solid gold ceremonial cannons cast to emit the honorific din. The cannons weighed two hundred and eighty pounds apiece. After which the argument as to how many times they were set off rather lost its point.

But then extravagance did rather run in the Baroda family. An earlier, less virtuous Gaekwar had taken to diamonds in a big way. In 1867 he bought the first great diamond to come out of the Brazilian mines. Known as the Star of the South, it cost Baroda £60,000 (£1,474,999 today) and was cut for him by Closter of Amsterdam. When the diamond arrived from Holland it was accorded a triumphal procession through the streets of Baroda in a sumptuous parade, complete with a saddled and bridled giraffe. Another Baroda diamond, the English Dresden, was of such a fierce white purity that when the Koh-i-noor was placed beside it it looked a trifle yellow.

Apart from collecting diamonds, the old Gaekwar encouraged somewhat bizarre manners at court — his farts and belches were greeted with rapturous applause by all who stood by, and should the prince yawn, all present would at once snap their fingers to discourage any fly that might otherwise have had the temerity to find its way into the royal mouth. The British viewed all this with superior calm, realizing that a prince who had erected in downtown

Bombay a fine white marble statue of the Queen-Empress could not be wholly bad.

But all display was as naught compared with the wealth of the Nizam of Hyderabad — known to gossip-column writers in the 1940s and 1950s as "the richest man in the world." (A title rather disputed by the Aga Khan, another Oriental potentate, whose faithful followers annually weighed him against a succession of precious substances, ranging from silver through to diamonds, which then became his to dispose of. The Aga Khan was not exactly slim — and the sums thus raised were enormous. The British, though impressed, nevertheless kept things in perspective. In the social register, invaluable to any society hostess, it listed him thus: "The Aga Khan is held to be a direct descendant of God. An English duke takes precedence.")

Nobody, however, neither hostess nor devoted follower, took the Nizam of Hyderabad to be anything but flesh and blood. He was the ruler of a kingdom as large as England and Scotland put together. A patriotic potentate, in order to show his enthusiasm for the British cause, the Nizam had raised an entire regiment to fight alongside the Tommies in the last war — a move motivated, perhaps, as much by a desire to fend off the nationalistic threats of the likes of Bose, as by an unadulterated admiration for the British Empire.

In most other things the Nizam was a man of modest tastes — he wore tattered clothes and smoked roll-ups. He kept a hoard of small coins about his person and frequently sent out for his meals to the bazaar. His jewels, however, were valued at three million pounds and after his death strong rooms full of bank notes were discovered, eaten through by rats. Also uncovered, and perhaps even more of a waste, were storerooms containing hundreds of cases of

Roger & Gallet soaps. Few boxes had been opened; the richest man in the world, it seemed, seldom took a bath.

*G*et Rich Quick

Not all great fortunes are gained by strictly honest means, and competitors — and on occasion the police — have been known to speak quite severely of the methods used by certain millionaires. "Unswervingly dishonest," for example, were the words applied to one railroad baron, while another was said to have "the morals of a gutter crocodile" — a reptile unknown, one suspects, to zoologists.

We are not concerned in this book with straight fraud — or with crooked fraud, for that matter; but the computer has given new meaning to the phrase "getting rich quick," and we can't resist a rapid glance at a particularly fine example of this phenomenon.

A computer wizard named Stanley Mark Rifkin was employed as a consultant by the Security Pacific National Bank of Los Angeles. His particular brief was to safeguard the customers' confidential accounts. It occurred to him that the best way to do this was to take charge of all the money in the bank — but *all* of it — himself. So on the evening of October 25, 1978, he picked up his hotline telephone and used the confidential computer codes with which he had been entrusted to transfer $18,145,000 to himself at a pseudonymous account in the Irving Trust Company of New York. It seems probable that this was the most quickly made $18,145,000 in history.

Unfortunately for Mr. Rifkin, he acquired an instant taste for bold and decisive financial moves, so on that very same night he used his new money to buy in Zurich a hundred and fifteen thousand Soviet diamonds. Alas, it had escaped his attention that other, and better, men before him had discovered that these diamonds were impossible to sell. He couldn't sell them, either—and he was duly apprehended when he tried to do so. Perhaps, as he languished in the state penitentiary, he took some comfort from the fact that the Security Pacific National Bank had no better luck with the diamonds. When they in their turn came to sell them, they took a massive loss.

Another spectacularly successful and remarkably ingenious fraud was perpetrated by a legendary inhabitant of Los Angeles. One day, when paying a modest sum into his sadly depleted account, he realized that should his personal computer sorting code be imprinted on all the blank

paying-in slips laid out for customers in a hurry to make a deposit, he would be extremely fortunate. Resolutely, he acted at once on the brain wave, and had thousands of slips printed bearing the magnetic code of his personal account. Then, at opening time, he went around to all the bank's many Los Angeles branches, substituting his private paying-in slips for the normal blanks. By evening, the obliging computer had paid all the day's takings for the Los Angeles area into his bank account. America's newest millionaire promptly drew out all the money and was never seen again.

If Music Be the Food of Love...

Ever since Blondel the page serenaded Richard Coeur de Lion, music has been among the privileges of the rich. Mad King Ludwig of Bavaria led in this field, as in many others. He simply hired Wagner as his personal composer and then sat all by himself—and furthermore rigidly awake—through entire performances of *Götterdämmerung*. But then, princes often are rather different from the rest of us.

Though not all that different from Sir Joseph Beecham (who was, after all, a king in the realm of patent medicine). When the Hallé orchestra was visiting his native St. Helen's and their conductor, Richter, took sick, Sir Joseph decreed that his son Tommy should take over the concert, and in the St. Helen's of 1899 nobody would have dreamed of arguing with the magnate, even if his lad had been unable to distinguish between a piccolo and a tuba.

As it turned out, Thomas Beecham's debut was good news for concertgoers, just as Captain John Christie's devotion to his wife was good news for opera lovers. In 1931 this Sussex landowner married the charming and talented soprano Audrey Mildmay. His love offering was to build her an opera house all of her own on his estate at Glyndebourne.

So much for love offerings. Less excitable rich people win their musical immortality as patrons. Who would have heard of the Esterhazys if they had not had the good sense to employ Haydn at their court (even if they were a bit mean about holidays)? And Archbishop Colloredo of Salzburg could not have become famous for having Mozart kicked downstairs if he had not first employed him — however reluctantly — as his court composer.

Mozart was buried in an unmarked pauper's grave, and Haydn was not a rich man when he died: but two makers of music, at least, were born to great wealth (not counting King Frederick the Great and King Henry VIII — both competent composers). The first of these two was the composer Lord Berners, an old Etonian whose family name was Tyrwhitt. He had a clavichord fitted into the back seat of his Rolls-Royce, so that he could relieve the boredom of long drives by composing this or that. Apart from a setting for *Du bist wie eine Blume* — a poem by Heine addressed to a small white pig — an "Elegy for a Rich Aunt" and another for a canary, Lord Berners wrote perfectly respectable ballets for Diaghilev in the twenties.

Florence Foster Jenkins, on the other hand, was seldom thought musically respectable even by her intimate friends. She was an immensely rich Newport hostess who saw herself as a greatly gifted dramatic soprano. For years she indulged herself by giving concerts at the Ritz-Carlton in New York. Her style might best be described as taking aim at a note with a scatter-gun and hoping against hope that she hit it. Her assembled friends and acquaintances would be observed swaying and ducking in breathless anticipation of whatever ear-shattering surprise was going to come next. Among Mrs. Jenkins's showpieces were the bell song from *Lakmé* and the Queen of the Night's aria from *The Magic Flute*, and strong men quite often wept at her performances of them. Her musical soirees became so famous that she was encouraged to launch herself on the general public, which she did at Carnegie Hall on October 25, 1944. People fell on the tickets in delirious expectation, and this and her subsequent concerts were sold out. No one ever hinted to Florence Foster Jenkins that true music lovers may have been thin on the ground at her recitals, though people sometimes wondered whether she knew all along. Whether she did or not, she maintained the grave manner of a great artiste to the end.

In more modern times pop star David Bowie had a Moog synthesizer built into his incandescent powder blue 1973 Lincoln Continental. This rolling retreat also rejoiced in a television set, paintings and a backseat hanging garden. Music on the move, as Lord Berners remarked, helps to shorten a dull journey remarkably.

*C*loser to God in a Garden

Jay Gould, who was in special need of closeness to his Maker, had one redeeming feature — his love of flowers. His special passion was the grandest of all flowers — the orchid. In an age when most sizable establishments sported green-houses growing orchids, the Robber Baron had the largest orchid houses in the world at his home, Lyndhurst. The exotic blooms came from far and wide — eight thousand varieties came from beyond Trebizond alone.

An army of highly qualified and educated gardeners looked after the plants — and were kept fully employed not only by the orchids, but by a collection of more than two thousand varieties of azalea. It is said that Jay Gould pre-ferred the company of the rare blooms he cultivated to that of human beings, whom he definitely did not cultivate.

In more recent times, a New York criminal lawyer with an enormously profitable practice, Paul D. Cravath, also had a passion for gardening. He, however, was a gardener of the indoor variety. Accordingly, when he had a $300,000 ($1,680,000 today) house built on the north shore of Long Island, he had a stream dammed up and then diverted so as to run through the middle of his home. The astonished architect, having realized that his client was above such mundane considerations as rising damp, simply asked what sort of stream was required. On being informed that the choice lay between "one that mutters, bubbles, mur-murs or purrs," the millionaire lawyer opted on the spot for

all four. The cost of the extra hydraulic engineering: $75,000 ($420,000 today).

Another modern millionaire, Calouste Gulbenkian, Mr. Five Percent himself, shared Jay Gould's passion for gardens, although he certainly also cultivated the human race at large with considerable abandon. In 1930 he bought a 150-acre garden near Deauville, at that time the most fashionable part of France. Here he set about the creation of an ideal garden — at the cost of some £500,000 (£8,380,681 today). Not only were trees brought from all over the world, but there were literally hundreds of different kinds of tropical birds shivering in the climate of northern France. Sixty gardeners worked full time to tend this unlikely paradise.

The only thing was that there was no house attached to the gardens. Their use for fashionable entertaining was, therefore, somewhat circumscribed. Their owner, however, used to come twice a year and stay in a hotel nearby so that he could take evening strolls. When asked whether the enormous cost of the upkeep was entirely justified by a couple of evenings of solitude every year, he said that it certainly was.

Castle in the Air

In June 1982, Malcolm Forbes, American millionaire publisher of the super-rich's own house magazine *Forbes*, approached the reliable Cameron Balloon Company of Bristol and commissioned a balloon shaped like his château in France, the Château Balleroy. The balloon, some hundred feet long by eighty feet high, was duly constructed and then released full of hot air into the stratosphere at the millionaire's annual balloon rally in Normandy. After the manner of the prudent super-rich, the inflatable château was tax deductible. The whole incident emphasized Mr. Forbes's determined attempt to overcome his own pessimistic dictum: "By the time we get it, we've had it."

*C*an't Give the StuffAway

Next to making money, the thing that most exercises the minds of some millionaires is how to give the stuff away. In some cases it's been how *not* to give their money to their children, a subspecies whom super-rich parents have often considered to be feckless wastrels, degenerates, idlers or worse. . . . In the light of this, millionaires' charity cannot be said to begin habitually at home. Which is just as well for the rest of us.

For instance, in the 1890s the fabulously rich Lady Houston used to tour the streets of Paris intent on good works, her handbag stuffed with gold sovereigns and large white five-pound notes. Today she would probably have been mugged. All that happened then was that she was surrounded by awed and importunate members of the lower classes.

In all Lady Houston probably only managed to give away a few thousand pounds. Her contemporary Alfred Nobel managed to give away millions.

A perfectly ordinary Norwegian armaments manufacturer, Alfred Nobel took to philanthropy when his brother died in 1888 and a Paris paper with Gallic enthusiasm published in error Alfred's own obituary. Given the rare experience of such a sneak preview, Alfred found himself described among other things as "a merchant of death." So shocked was he, that he instantly founded the Nobel Academy in order to give substantial cash prizes to those who had done most to advance mankind—rather than simply kill them off, as his products had done. The prizes were to be for medicine, peace, literature and so forth—and caught on like wildfire with public and laureates alike.

Thus Nobel was immortalized as what he fundamentally was not—a benefactor of mankind; and he is not alone among donating millionaires in encouraging good works in areas remote from their own activities.

For instance, Cecil Rhodes (qv), who captured much of the world's gold as well as the hinterland of Africa, gave his entire vast fortune to the cause of higher education—something which he himself had never had. Generations of Rhodes scholars, however, praise his philanthropy—and Rhodes's name, amazingly considering the man, has become synonymous with learning and civilized values.

Another self-educated man who took to supporting education in a truly princely fashion was steel baron Andrew Carnegie (qv), who was born in a small farm in Scotland in 1835. He traveled to America where he fast became one of the world's richest men. But no sooner did Carnegie become rich than he embarked on a concerted plan to get rid of the filthy stuff. The trouble was the more he gave away the more he made—so in the end the mere business of giving away had grown into a multimillion-dollar business requiring yet another entire corporate staff.

Libraries were Carnegie's first love—and he began in Scotland, a nation he apparently felt to be peculiarly in need of literacy and learning. Carnegie took to giving away books as a duck to water—and in the end he had endowed two thousand eight hundred and eleven free libraries in the United States, the United Kingdom, Canada, New Zealand, South Africa, the Seychelles, Mauritius and the Islands of Fiji. The total cost to Carnegie: $50,364,808 ($280,000,000 today).

From literature Carnegie turned to music. On one occasion he visited a church with his father, and finding that it lacked an organ, naturally donated one. Within weeks he was inundated with requests for more of them. By 1919 Carnegie had given away seven thousand six hundred and eighty-nine organs. The cost of this particular piece of doing-good-noisily: $6,242,312 ($34,956,947 today).

Even giving on such a scale had no effect on Carnegie's overall wealth. When he died the press fanned public speculation as to how much the billionaire had left — and to whom. In the event, Andrew Carnegie left $350,695,652 ($1,960,000,000 today). He was not, however, disgraced by this as he had feared, since his wealth was clearly too vast for any man, however diligent, to spend; and in any case, nine-tenths of it was left to further his good works.

Carnegie, like Rhodes and Nobel, gained enormous fame and reputation by his charitable enthusiasms. Other millionaires preferred to do good genuinely by stealth. A striking example, the Newmarket television rental millionaire, David Robinson, gave seventy-five million pounds to a Cambridge college that was to bear his name — on condition that he didn't have to show up at the opening ceremony, even though it was due to be performed by the Queen. . . .

But perhaps one of the most extraordinary givers of modern times was the American computer millionaire C. Ross Perot, who made untold millions in computer-leasing in the 1960s. Looking around for a suitable way of serving the community, Mr. Perot decided that he would give a Christmas present to every American prisoner-of-war in Vietnam. Accordingly, thousands of parcels were wrapped and packed, and a fleet of Boeing 707s was chartered to deliver them to Hanoi. Then the message came from the government of Vietnam — no such gesture could be considered during the course of the bloody war, which was then at its height. Perot argued. The Vietnamese replied that any charity was impossible while American B-52s were devastating Vietnamese villages.

"No problem," Perot replied. He would hire an expert American construction company in order to rebuild anything the Americans had knocked down.

The puzzled Vietnamese became inscrutable, and declined to continue this dialogue. Christmas drew closer; the parcels remained undelivered. Finally in despair Perot took off in his chartered fleet and flew to Moscow where his aides posted the parcels, one at a time, at the Moscow Central post office. They were delivered intact.

Setting the World to Rights

Everybody has heard sinister stories of political millionaires using their vast wealth and cunning to subvert the will of nations to their own benefit. After the death of President Kennedy there were many such stories claiming the assassination to be due to a conspiracy on behalf of the extreme right, and based in Texas. At the time nothing was proved — and indeed the whole idea still seems pretty improbable to those who are not conspiratorially minded. What is true, however, is that Fritz von Thyssen, chairman of the United Steel works in Germany, not only subsidized Adolf Hitler in the 1920s to the tune of a hundred thousand gold marks, but proudly proclaimed it in his memoirs which he even entitled: *"I Paid Hitler."*

Also often proclaimed — although a good deal less seriously — is the fact that the extreme right in England, initially known as the League of Empire Loyalists, received its original funding from an eccentric millionaire in South America, one Robert K. Jeffery, who kept two baths full of walnuts, a food that he held to be vital to human life and soon to become mysteriously subject to a world shortage.

Another vastly rich and politically minded millionaire was the late Duke of Bedford who regularly sponsored candidates for Parliament during the 1950s in the interest of the Duke of Bedford's British Patriotic Party, which aimed for a society all British, white and anti-Communist. One of its major platforms was that His Grace was the

48

rightful monarch of England. The Duke of Bedford's party tended to poll a substantial number of votes only in constituencies that embraced the Bedford estates.

Nor are irrational views held only by fringe millionaires. No less a figure than Henry Ford was known to hold anti-Semitic views. He published a series of demagogic articles in his journal, *The Dearborn Independent*, starting with the issue of May 22, 1920, which carried a front-page story entitled: "The International Jew: The World's Problem." The series ran for ninety issues — until 1927 when Henry Ford had a change of heart and recanted and then folded his propaganda paper.

Another billionaire who believed that he alone knew how to put the world to rights was H. L. Hunt, the Texan oilman and father of Bunker and Lamar Hunt. His creed was simple: he believed that every citizen should have voting power according to how much tax he paid. Rather than publish a newspaper in order to propagate these rather undemocratic views, H. L. Hunt took to fiction — possibly the best medium for such a message — and penned the novel *Alpaca*. It did not sell well, members of the public seemingly only buying it according to how much tax they paid.

*B*low Out

One appetite that the super-rich share with even the poor is . . . well, appetite. Although even in this field, the old adage, "the rich *are* different," has some force.

Consider for instance the eighteenth century millionaire, Lord Alvanley, whose obsession in life was apricot tarts. Every day his chef was instructed to make one — in an age when apricots were not to be found on the shelves of every downtown supermarket. Woe betide the poor fellow if he managed to clothe the confection in soggy pastry, since his lordship's wrath was dreadful to behold.

One day Lord Alvanley ran a contest in his club, White's in St. James's, to see which of his fellow clubmen could invent the most expensive dish. All over London chefs labored over hot stoves, topped by bubbling copper vats filled with truffles and turtles and larks' tongues. Not surprisingly, since he had set the ground rules, his lordship won his own contest with a fricassee of *noix*, taken from no less than thirteen types of birds. The final dish included the meat of three hundred birds — including a hundred snipe, forty woodcock and twenty pheasants. The cost of the dish eaten by the assembled contestants — £108.5s.

Lord Alvanley liked savories; his contemporary Sir John Irwin, the lord lieutenant of Dublin, had a sweet tooth. Once, to mark a special occasion, he had a cake baked for him that was designed as a scale model of the rock of Gibraltar, complete with the fortress on top, all constructed of suitably colored sugar. There was even artillery, made to

51

scale, which threw sugar plums as cannon balls against the glacé walls of the sugar citadel. The cost of this rock folly: £1,500. In the circumstances it is hardly surprising that Sir John had to end his days in France, where he had fled to avoid his creditors. France is the land of pastry cooks, so let us hope Sir John died a satiated man.

Consider also Lord North, the sixteenth century ancestor of the Lord North to whom Americans owe their freedom. In 1577 he invited his queen, Elizabeth the First, to pay a three-day visit to his estates. During their stay the queen and her party munched their way through sixty-seven sheep, thirty-four pigs, four stags, sixteen bucks — who collectively went to make up a hundred and seventy-five pasties — one thousand two hundred chickens, three hundred and sixty-three capons, thirty-three geese, two hundred and thirty-seven dozen pigeons, one entire cartload of oxen, and then, when supplies ran out, two horse-loads of oysters, three thousand five hundred eggs, and four hundred and thirty pounds of butter.

On a somewhat more modest scale, a more modern ruler, namely President Theodore Roosevelt, was a great trencherman. Visitors to the presidential mansion at Sagamore Hill observed with awe the presidential eating habits. For instance, for breakfast the president wolfed down an entire fried chicken in white sauce before he began the day. And above all, the president had a sweet tooth — he took seven spoonfuls of sugar in his morning coffee — fortunately, in an era before the powers of the Food and Drug Administration had grown to such a point that they could stamp it out.

Twice the Man

Not many women have been millionaires in their own right—but those that have made their pile have done it with great style and verve.

One of the earliest examples—always excepting a series of formidable customers in the comely shapes of such queens as Catherine the Great and Elizabeth the First—is Angela Burdett Coutts, the granddaughter of Thomas Coutts, a canny Scot who became the utterly discreet and utterly rich banker to the royal family. Angela inherited the whole lot when her eccentric grandmother died and became the richest and thus the most eligible young woman in Victorian England. However, she would have none of her suitors—turning down in quick succession Louis Napoleon and King Leopold of the Belgians. She also declined the advances of White Rajah Brooke of Sarawak. On this occasion, although Miss Coutts remained steadfast in her determination not to be history's first white ranee, the foreign secretary was informed by the Foreign Office that her suitability for the job was "greatly enhanced by the fact that she was the State's principal creditor."

Having turned down these assorted thrones, Miss Coutts made a pair of propositions herself—one to the Iron Duke of Wellington, the other to Charles Dickens. Both turned her down with due expressions of regret—the Duke, after all, was seventy-eight and felt himself unequal to even so profitable a last engagement.

Jilted, the millionairess took to good works with frantic vigor, establishing bishoprics here and there in the colonies, seeing to the dreadfully unfashionable needs of unmarried mothers, worrying about London's sewage system and frustrating the speculative builders on Hampstead Heath. These, as well as sundry other good works, she did mainly by stealth, which earned her the nickname of "Lady Unknown."

However, Angela Coutts did not have to wait for heaven for her rewards. They came on earth — she was created the first baroness in her own right to sit in the House of Lords, the first freewoman of the City of London, and in due time, was buried in Westminster Abbey.

But before that happy end, Lady Coutts gained a more material reward. At the age of sixty-seven she married a youth of twenty-seven — and an American to boot. When "society" expressed its outrage, Lady Coutts is said to have exclaimed: "Had I been a man of sixty-seven marrying a girl forty years my junior it would have been a matter of universal congratulations."

Equally rich, but infinitely less attractive, was the nineteenth century's other leading millionairess — Hetty Green of New England. Inheriting ten million dollars from her father at the age of thirty, Hetty succeeded in parlaying it into many times that sum. Her father had taught her that all men were not only beasts but also golddiggers — perhaps in her case with some reason. Anyway, Hetty did her best to fend off unwelcome suitors by going about unwashed and dressed in rags. Finally, as so often is the case, she married a man as rich as herself — only to divorce him the instant he committed the unpardonable crime of losing all his money and, to compound matters, expected his wife to make good his debts. After this unpleasing episode she took to going from doss house to flophouse dressed in black rags, dragging her unwilling children with her. Popular journalists called her "The Witch of Wall

Street," and a biographer wrote: "In spending money she might be compared with an athlete who never broke training."

True to form she resold empty medicine bottles, and after reading the morning papers would send her son out to resell them. When the aforesaid son dislocated his knee-cap falling off his sled, she refused at first to get him a doctor, and then dressed them both in paupers' dress so as to get free treatment at a destitutes' hospital. By the time proper help could be summoned the boy had to have his leg amputated. In spite of the resulting savings in shoe leather, he rather turned against his mother. By way of revenge, when he finally inherited a half share in Hetty's one hundred million dollar estate ($560,000,000 today) he blew the lot — showing a special penchant for underage girls and yachts.

After such a start, not surprisingly the next generation or two of millionairesses showed slightly less flair. It is true that the new-found profession of couturier made it possible for a number of women to make rather than inherit their fortunes — and Coco Chanel and Helena Rubinstein were among the super-rich businesswomen who rode to fame and fortune on the backs, as it were, of their sisters. But the lady who made the most impression on popular imagination between the wars and later was Barbara Hutton, who inherited a cool, or rather a cozy, twenty million dollars ($148,000,000 today) from her grandfather, Frank Woolworth, on her twenty-first birthday in 1930. She celebrated the event with a modest celebration which cost a mere sixty thousand dollars ($327,485 today) — held at the Ritz Carlton in New York. This happy event safely out of the way, Ms. Hutton took to collecting husbands with some vigor and enthusiasm. Her first was Prince Alexis Mdivani, although technically she didn't wait until her coming-of-age before tying the knot, since the heiress was only twenty years old at the time. Anyway, after due settlement the keen collector moved on to Count Kurt von Haugwitz-Reventlow. This second noble match lasted nine years, after which Ms. Hutton moved on to the nobility of Hollywood, allowing Cary Grant to lead her to the altar in 1942. Beverly Hills wags dubbed them "Cash and Cary." Four years later she dropped the elegant parcel off and married Prince Igor Troubetzkoy, who doubtless led Ms. Hutton a heady dance. Four years later he too was given the chop, to be succeeded in double quick time by playboy—his semiofficial title— Porfirio Rubirosa: a marriage that lasted a modest seventy-two days. Somewhat lowering her aristocratic sights, Ms. Hutton then got hitched to a German tennis ace, a mere Baron von Cramm. Five years later they too were divorced, leaving the field clear for an Indo-Chinese, Prince Doan Vinh. By this time the lady's stamina was clearly giving out, because when this marriage ended in 1975 it was merely by separation, not divorce.

Maybe that was all to the good—Ms. Hutton's divorces and above all her life-style proved to be a remarkable drain even on a fortune calculated in 1939 at $319 million ($2,147 million today). Prince Alexis—first in—got one million dollars on marriage as a sort of dowry, and then another two million to go away. Count Kurt also received a million-dollar dowry—and a mere one and a half million dollars on divorce, perhaps a trifle mean when one considers that he had asked for five million. Cary Grant got nothing—not being exactly on the breadline himself. Prince Igor didn't do so well either and had the temerity to take the lady to court. For his pains they charged him three hundred dollars in court fees and gave him nothing. As he left the court, he would have done well to ponder the words of Kin Hubbard: "Nobody works as hard for his money as the man who marries it."

Richer Than Croesus

Croesus gains a place in any book on millionaires by virtue of having given his name to the state of super-richness. The protobillionaire was the last king of Lydia and ruled from 560 B.C. to 546 B.C. His territorial ambitions embraced the capture of as much of the known world as possible. Croesus set about achieving this with some vigor, only to fall foul of Cyrus the Great who pursued him back to his capital city, Sardis.

After a prolonged and savage siege, the city was sacked and King Croesus captured. He was sentenced to death by Cyrus — but such was the way of things that in the nick of time Apollo wafted him away from the executioners' pyre and transported him by air to Egypt.

So much is legend. The truth is that modern archaeological diggings in Lydia have uncovered vast smelting and refining factories given over to the production of the civilized world's first gold coins. Making Croesus, one supposes, a sort of early disciple of Professeur Rueff, who ensured the financial health of France in the 1960s by his addiction to gold.

The Further They Fall

America is always claiming to be the home of the best and the biggest in all fields of human endeavor; but in one such field — that of bankruptcy — the Old Country leaves the New World far behind. The world record holder is William George Stern, a British property tycoon who went up the tubes for a mere £104,390,248. Curiously enough this extraordinary debacle did little to change Mr. Stern's style of life.

"Bankruptcy is not a universal leveler," he remarked — and indeed his house, his pictures and his Rolls-Royce car all turned out to be owned by his family trust, and the trustees in their wisdom allowed him to continue in the enjoyment thereof. Perhaps, given such magnificent support. Stern may eventually be able to devote a little more than £6,000 a year to settling his debts. That is his original offer, which means that many of his creditors will have to wait seventeen thousand years to be paid off in full.

"As Far As the Eye Can See . . ."

"This land is mine," the Old Earl said. Thus spoke the Earl of Dorincourt, in the immortal pages of *Little Lord Fauntleroy*. His was a good, resounding boast. The Countess of Sutherland could make it too, if she so wished, for she is one of the largest landowners in Great Britain, mistress of some 100,000 acres, and it would take long sight to see across that. The only trouble is that most of those acres are in the remotest highlands and are of far more interest to red deer than to property speculators. They are good, however, for impressing the grandchildren.

There are — or have been — landholdings in Europe belonging to princely families that are much larger. Once upon a time the Radziwills, for example, had estates in Poland centered on Potocki that covered 6,500 square miles, about half the size of Ireland. Great estates such as those of the Sutherland and the Radziwill families have passed from generation to generation for so long that they seem always to have belonged to them, but presumably they were originally acquired by conquest and by alliance-making, or parts of them were bestowed on some intrepid ancestor as a reward for winning a critical battle.

That last process can be seen in the case of the Duke of Wellington. He got both the battlefield of Waterloo — generously interpreted — and the lines of Torres Vedras in Spain as a "thank-you," and his descendants still do quite well from these acquisitions, in spite of the fact that the grateful governments of the Iron Duke's day have been succeeded by governments a good deal less grateful. Indeed the present Belgian government expends a good deal of energy trying to persuade today's Iron Duke to give some of it back. But short of another battle of Waterloo ...

Being given a little bit of someone else's land is one thing, but taking a whole country for yourself is quite another. In modern times very few people have managed it, and those who brought it off were justifiably proud.

Consider Cecil Rhodes. A weedy boy from Bishops Stortford, he was sent to Africa at the age of eighteen for the good of his health. It was hoped that the climate would suit him. And indeed it did. It suited him so well and stimulated him so briskly that within a couple of years he had become one of the richest men in the world. He started by cornering the water rights for all the diamond digs in Kimberley, and having thereby extracted vast sums from the miners, he then set about buying up the digs. Finally he bought the Kimberley Tip—the largest diamond mine in the world—from Barney Barnato, for a bucketful of diamonds and membership in the Kimberley club (Barnato was a Jew, and the club excluded Jews). That done, Rhodes raised an army and carved a new nation out of the heart of Africa.

Since an army was necessary for such an undertaking, it should have been obvious to everyone that Africa was not at all keen on being carved, and that there were people about who were under the impression that they were nations already; but it was generally supposed that these people were misguided and that they would start appreciating the good fortune that had come their way as soon as they settled down to being citizens of ... of what? What was this new nation to be called? Casting round for a suitable name, Rhodes hit by some strange chance on Rhodesia.

A far less bustling Victorian, though no less acquisitive, was a sea-dog of Scottish descent named Captain

Clunies-Ross. In 1827 he chanced to land on one of the Cocos Islands — there are some twenty-seven of them altogether — whereupon he simply took possession of the lot, in the name not of his country but of himself. In 1886 Queen Victoria generously confirmed the family's ownership of these islands that had nothing to do with her, and from then on the Clunies-Rosses simply ruled the place as "kings of the Cocos." It was not until 1975 that anybody paid much attention to this toy-town kingdom, when the faraway Australian government decided to stamp out this leftover anomaly of colonialism and feudal tyranny. By that time its current holder had crowned himself King John and was striding barefoot round his realm in a kilt, complete with dirk in belt. Not surprisingly, he was less than keen on giving up his bit of feudalism and selling out to the Australian government, nor were his six hundred subjects very happy at the change. They had become accustomed to their royal family — and to being paid the equivalent of twopence a day in the form of a plastic token. Who needs change, they said, if they live in a place not far from being paradise, with endless beaches, no loud music and only one crime a year? But, alas, such romantic olde-worlde considerations count for little to the tidy bureaucratic mind, and today the plastic tokens are worth only their weight in plastic.

Rhodes, Clunies-Ross and Stamford Raffles, the founding father of Singapore — each of them created his own country in his own way. But their achievements look almost paltry beside that of the only man who ever bought a whole empire for money, and then gave it away to a friend. This man was Jakob Fugger, justly known as "the rich." Fugger succeeded where Bunker Hunt failed, and cornered a commodity: copper, in his case. Fifteenth century Augsburg was a prosperous place, but even there Fugger stood out as being very very rich. Some of his well-gotten gains he spent on purchasing the Holy Roman Empire, which he gave to

Charles V. He paid 544,000 guilders for it — the underbidder, King Francis I of France, was able to raise no more than 310,000. So different has life become during the intervening centuries that it is pretty well impossible to guess at modern equivalents of these astronomic sums.

With the coming of the twentieth century the take-over of whole nations — to say nothing of empires — by private citizens came to be rather frowned upon. One man, however, is rich enough still so to do. His name: Daniel K. Ludwig. In order to find something to occupy his old age this eighty-four-year-old shipping billionaire — regularly tipped for the title of "the richest man in the world" — decided to build a personal empire in what had hitherto been considered impenetrable Brazilian rain forest. To this end he invested a billion dollars in homesteading the Amazonian jungle. Among the civil engineering projects the scheme necessitated were the construction of 4,800 kilometers of roads and forty-one kilometers of railroad. Thirty thousand people came to live in Ludwig's dream enclave, forty-eight hours by boat from the nearest Amazonian port.

Unfortunately, the whole thing seems to have been a total washout — literally — owing to the inclement weather. It says a good deal for Mr. Ludwig's resources that he could lose all this in the forests of Brazil without anyone — but anyone — thinking to suggest for a moment that it remotely endangers his billionaire-plus status.

Words of Wisdom

Gambling and philanthropy apart, the very rich don't often rush to give away much in the way of material goods — one of the reasons, no doubt, why they stay very rich. From time to time, however, they let slip a piece of advice. If picked up by the right person at the right moment, it can work.

For example, one afternoon at the turn of the last century a young actress named Eleanor Robson, who had just arrived from Los Angeles, was walking down Beacon Street in Boston. As she passed number 152 she heard someone rapping at a window, looked up and saw a parlormaid beckoning her urgently to the front door. Could she have an unknown fan at this address, she wondered, as she bounded up the steps. The imposing door swung open to reveal the mistress of the house, Isabella Stewart Gardner, who was a society hostess of enormous wealth and considerable renown.

"Walk erect, young woman!" ordered this formidable old lady, whereupon, without another word, the door swung shut.

This oracular instruction impressed Eleanor so deeply that she became a very model of deportment and thereby soon caught the eye of August Belmont Jr., the multimillionaire banker. Their marriage placed her in circumstances to which she had not been accustomed, but this didn't bother her at all. As she remarked in her memoirs: "A private railroad car is not an acquired taste. One takes to it immediately."

Behind Every Successful Man . . .

For the wives of millionaires it is not balancing the house-keeping budget that presents a problem. It is finding something to spend it on. For instance Grace Williams, who married Cornelius Vanderbilt III, once in an idle moment worked out that every year for upward of fifty years she had spent some three hundred thousand dollars on entertaining her friends. Her total bill for glad-handing, therefore, must have worked out at something around fifteen million dollars ($78,000,000 today).

Maybe the millionaire's wife with the most developed instincts in this field in recent times was Gloria Rubio, the wife of the financier Loel Guinness, whose father had died in 1947 leaving him upward of two hundred million dollars ($1,040,000,000 today). Gloria, who had come from a penniless Mexican family, forthwith set about what she conceived to be her primary task: delighting the millionaire she had acquired. She spent on clothes with extraordinary vigor, proclaiming in tones that would not appeal to all her sisters today: "A woman's job is to please a man—I dress accordingly." Asked by the press if she had a hobby, Gloria Guinness replied: "Yes, one. Myself."

Another lady equally self-centered—and equally extravagant—was Eva Duarte who came to be known as Eva Perón or simply Evita, the strong woman of the Argen-

tine. She ordered her dresses by the military planeload
from Dior in Paris and often boasted that she had never
worn any dress twice. Eva began her life in poverty and
caught her dictator's eye after making a career as an actress
(though the techniques for which she was renowned were
not primarily those of the theater).

Plenty of people in the Argentine knew Evita's origins (although uncomfortable things were likely to happen to them if they said as much), but the model Nina Dyer, who flourished in the 1950s, seemed to come from nowhere. In 1954 she married the German steel magnate Baron Heini von Thyssen. The happy couple separated ten months later. In spite of the brevity of the encounter, Nina received a generous divorce settlement of two and a half million dollars and an island named "Tiamo" ("I love you" in Italian). Among the knickknacks she also retained were a three-row necklace of a hundred and fifty-one exquisite black pearls, later sold for half a million dollars, and several assorted motor cars.

Nina did not remain inconsolable for long, nor did her next husband, Prince Sadruddin, half-brother of the Aly Khan, represent a fall in her standard of living. They parted in 1960, and on this occasion the lady received a further half a million dollars. Shortly afterward she committed suicide by taking an overdose of sleeping tablets, although nobody seemed to know why.

Reporters at Nina's funeral noted that the casket was covered in two million dollars' worth of red roses, a gift from her two ex-husbands, and at the same time something of a unique testimonial.

Nina's settlements seem almost modest by today's standards. Indeed Britain itself has produced one contender for the title of the most expensive divorce claim of all time. In the red-white-and-blue corner: Sandra Jarvis-Daley, born in a humble terrace house in Leicester. Her husband: Arab financier Adnan Khashoggi, much loved by gossip columnists and others for his jet-set life-style and mysterious Arab business activities.

Mrs. Khashoggi, when filing for divorce in California in August 1979, claimed a mere billion pounds — plus an extra £279 million for the inconvenience and the small matter of legal fees. As it turned out, her caution about Californian legal fees was well founded. Months after a private settlement, she was still being pursued by her own lawyers for a trifling £206,000.

High Rollers

It seems extraordinary that millionaires who have made piles of money the hard way should enjoy the act of losing it — and losing it, what's more, in a manner that everyone knows favors the casino. But apparently it is the plunge from elation to despair and back again that is so addictive in gambling, so perhaps for a millionaire the emotional roller coaster seems cheap at the price.

The first really impressive wager on record was made by that lady of all the pleasures, Cleopatra, in the year 1 B.C. At dinner one night the wily oriental queen bet Mark Antony that she could drink half a million dollars' worth of wine without even getting up from the orgying table. He, poor thing, must have already had his wits dimmed by the Egyptian equivalent of before-dinner martinis, because he took the bet — only to find that Cleopatra had slinkily slipped a couple of pearls of the agreed value into the cup she had just quaffed. Cleopatra collected in full.

Although before he was through Mark Antony certainly qualified as one of the world's great losers, he was less remarkable as a gambler than many lesser men. There was an eighteenth century gambler so compulsively addicted that he once bet a vast sum on which of two raindrops would first reach the bottom of a window in his club in St. James's. He lost — which Beau Brummel emphatically did not do when he bet his host at a shooting party that at the end of the day he would have a heavier bag than any other gun in the field. Knowing that the Beau was very much greater as a wit and a man of fashion than he was as a shot, his host took him on. Brummel, as expected, did poorly with the birds — but calmly gunned down and bagged his host's liver-colored pointer bitch on the way home. Even so, it was a damned close-run thing — but in the end the host lost both the bitch and the bet.

A strange pile of masonry at Brightling in Kent commemorates another unusual wager. The mysterious construction was erected by one Jack Fuller who, in his London club, idly bet a fellow member that the spire of Dallington church could be seen from his drawing-room window. The wager was a thousand guineas (£26,702 today). Fuller must have been more familiar with his club than with his own house, because it turned out that in fact the spire was not visible from that window. Rather than lose his bet, he promptly had the church heightened by forty feet.

Bets on raindrops, church spires and such stick in people's minds because of their oddity, but in terms of the sums wagered they pale into insignificance beside the enormous amounts expended by nineteenth century swells on horse racing — a sport which seems to have existed solely to give people something to bet on. Lord George Bentinck, for instance, once lost £26,000 on a single race — and, nothing abashed, went on to build Goodwood racecourse, the better to lose more.

Another punter — like Bentinck a millionaire to start with — did rather better out of Goodwood, for it was at this Sussex racecourse that Bet-a-Million Gates earned his name. Actually, it was not a million in the currency of the day that this American billionaire won on his horse Royal Flush, when it came first in the Stewards' Cup, but a mere $600,000. By the standards of the day this sum was enormous, but Bet-Six-Hundred-Thousand Gates doesn't have much ring to it, so a million it became. Anyway, Gates — who had invented barbed wire, which, at the time, proved useful for keeping Texan cattle in and later would prove equally useful for keeping enemy soldiers out—was what today is called a compulsive gambler. Indeed, he once broke some kind of a gambling speed record, which he may well still hold today. On the occasion in question, Bet-a-Million was getting out of his coach in Main Street, Kansas City, when a man approached him and offered to wager $40,000 on the spin of a coin. Gates accepted, tossed and won, all in the space of ten seconds. When he died, taking a last gamble as to his final destination, Bet-a-Million left a fortune in excess of fifty million dollars. Few gamblers are so fortunate.

Stories of spectacular losses are more common in the annals of gambling than stories of success, but quite recently twenty-three-year-old M. Tadev Resende of Volta Redonda in Brazil had a nice stroke of luck. In February 1981, he won $3,003,532 in the Lotteria Sportiva. And a late entry—although the strictest application of the rules might exclude her from this modest book since she is $440 short of the required million: just as we went to press, on October 15, 1982, news came to us from Atlantic City of the great good luck of Ms. Alberta Joyce Kidd. This forty-nine-year-old mother of six won $999,559 on a slot machine. There is a complication, however: she was using her welfare check as stake money. To whom does the million bucks belong—the welfare department or America's newest millionairess? The debate continues. . . .

There was one bet that only the natural prudence of the gambler David Threlfall prevented from being so spectacularly successful as to make him a millionaire. For it was Mr. Threlfall who in 1964 obtained odds of a thousand to one that man would never walk on the surface of the moon. On July 21, 1969—five years later—he sat in a television studio with his bookie watching the Apollo Mission. Even before

Neil Armstrong actually took his great step forward for mankind the bookie handed the gambler a check for ₤10,000. "We know when we are beaten," the bookie proclaimed. A sentiment all too seldom to be heard on the lips of those hard men — often themselves millionaires.

Meanwhile, whenever Mr. Threlfall gets to wishing he had invested more than a ₤10 stake, he can always console himself with the wise old racetrack adage: "Nobody ever bet enough on a winning horse."

One of the earliest men to have a successful system was a French nineteenth century engineer. William Jaggens — although his rather unorthodox method might not have been all that welcome at Crockfords, since it involved six nongambling assistants who watched the tables all evening and made copious notes before M. Jaggens bet a sou. The wily Frenchie never actually told anybody what he was looking for, so his secret, which made him over one and a half million francs in a day and a half, died with him.

Of course, no account of those who earn their living by the precarious laws of chance would be complete without a mention of the late Nicholas Andrea Dandalos, otherwise Nick the Greek. A legend in our own time, Nick the Greek managed to turn the tables at Vegas by actually getting the casinos to pay *him* to stick around and play. It says something for his pulling power with lesser gamblers that he was tolerated at all since, in the course of a long career as a "gambling man," Nick won nearly six and a half million dollars a year at the race track. All in all, so he claimed, some five hundred million dollars actually passed through his hands — and a large number stuck to them. Perhaps the secret of his continued welcome at Vegas lay in the fact that he had been stony-broke no less than seventy-three times — always, of course, wagering his way back to his rightful millionairedom.

But perhaps the person to bring this section to an end is Garry Llewellyn of Des Moines, Iowa, who cannot really have set out to exemplify the perils of gambling, but certainly managed to do so. In 1982 the thirty-three-year-old Mr. Llewellyn "removed" fifteen million dollars from his daddy's bank and blew it in Vegas. By the time the bank became aware of its loss, some months had passed, and every cent had been frittered away beyond recall. Brought to trial, Mr. Llewellyn was found insane by reason of being a compulsive gambler.

A **Hint of Middle Eastern Promise**

In the late sixties, a well-connected and very young journalist on the London *Evening Standard* found himself between planes in the Gulf of Arabia. He decided to improve the shining hour by visiting one of the ruling sheikhs, hoping for enough copy to produce a feature article on his return to London. He arrived at a dusty palace and was kept waiting, and waiting, and waiting. Finally, the young man was summoned into the princely presence and a satisfactory interview ensued. On leaving, however, the very young journalist remarked that he had now missed his connection. His host expressed polite horror and offered to have him driven to the next principality — at whose airport the flight would be refueling. When they reached the airport the driver handed the journalist the keys of the car. The journalist handed them back. The driver returned them: "His Highness wishes to make up to you for the inconvenience — the Cadillac is yours." The plane was revving up on the tarmac — what to do? With a sigh the young man returned the keys to the suddenly enriched chauffeur — and caught the flight back to Heathrow, and his secondhand MG.

Fifteen years later another Arab prince — this time a Saudi — ended a visit to London by giving the temporary English chauffeur who had seen to his every need while driving him around the West End the keys to his Rolls-Royce Corniche.

By such gestures did the Arabs announce the birth of a great new wealth. Petromillionaires proved to be as unashamedly spendthrift as the maharajahs of a generation before. The jewelers and the nightclubs of London benefited right royally—as did Harley Street and the London Clinic. Sheikh Rashid, ruler of Dubai, once bought no less than one hundred pairs of £700 cuff links on one visit to a Bond Street jeweler—to say nothing of five white gold and diamond Piaget watches at £20,000. His total bill for the visit: £800,000. For princes requiring more military gifts the gunmakers James Purdey and Sons actually have a waiting list for gold-inlaid shotguns at £20,000 a matched pair.

All this, of course, came from the great new explosion of oil wealth—masterminded by Sheikh Yamani, the Saudi oil minister and the most famous Arab in the world. Developed nations, it has been said, quail at his word. Perhaps the most stunning manifestation of his power came when Harrods stayed open for him after hours so he could do a trifling amount of his Christmas shopping uninterrupted, a privilege normally reserved for members of the British royal family. Yamani spent a mere £35,000, had his chosen presents gift-wrapped and, finding that the pile of parcels would not fit into the trunk of his Rolls, stopped a passing coal truck and rewarded the driver sufficiently to persuade him to carry the surplus to Heathrow.

Another fabulously rich Saudi—who is not actually a prince—is Adnan Khashoggi, often described as an arms dealer. His yacht, and his wife's idea of an equitable divorce settlement, have already found their place in our pages. His DC-10 has not. Like the great pleasure-boats of bygone generations, it has the regulation Sienna marble bath with gold taps. It also has a double bed with a glass roof, so that the drowsy millionaire can count the clouds as they float by. The same transparency is to be found in the breakfast cabin—where the coffee table rests on an observation panel that again gives it an impression of floating through

the clouds, complete, no doubt, with silver linings. . . . On one occasion Khashoggi even used a second aircraft to transport his chosen mineral water to fill up his aerial bath.

But the real oil riches lie in the hands of the Saudi royal family. Saudi Arabia and Liechtenstein are the only two countries named after the royal families who govern them. Saudi Arabia has no budget, since everything in the country belongs to the crown. In a sense, this makes Saudi Arabia the only family firm represented at the United Nations. The previous king, Khaled, imported the best of everything into the country, including a giant water spout, modeled — though on a larger scale — on that in Lake Geneva, which his majesty had watched while undergoing rejuvenating treatment in a clinic in the Swiss city.

Recently, King Khaled's successor, King Fahd, visited a new ultramodern hotel for its opening party in Jeddah. He enjoyed himself regally, and was much pleased. He then made the startled owners an offer they could not refuse and purchased the whole place as a guest palace for his visitors.

At the same time a remote cousin of the king decided he needed a house in Hollywood and startled even the not-exactly-conservative though determinedly lovable people of Beverly Hills, by what he did to a magnificent old-style Hollywood palace. Not only did the princeling gild the roof and install terraces of technicolor plastic flowers, but — final insult — he painted the pubic hair of the tasteful eighteenth-century-style garden statues. The outraged, and by now slightly less lovable, neighbors got up petitions and counterpetitions — a local drama that came to a rather anticlimactic end when a mysterious fire gutted the whole place and propelled its aberrant owner off to cause further havoc in Miami.

Meanwhile back in London, as we go to press, a Kuwaiti financier holds the current record for losses at the gaming tables. His deficit to date: £28 million.

*G*olden Meanies

Until recently the richest man in England was said to be Sir John Ellerman, a shipping tycoon so wealthy that it was always claimed that when he died income tax would go down to ninepence on the pound. (Upon his demise in July 1973 the grief of his fellow citizens was not, alas, moderated by any such happy event.) During his lifetime, Sir John (who shared with Harry Hyams of Centre Point fame a horror of being photographed) made a habit of traveling on his own boats as a steerage passenger. It was after one of these trips, it is said, that he decreed that the lavatory cisterns on all the ships of the Ellerman Line be forthwith converted from fresh-water to salt-water flushing in order to effect a meaningful economy in operating costs.

Such careful husbandry would have appealed to another contemporary millionaire, Paul Getty. The oilman became a legend in his own time for his meanness. Getty would never leave a meeting first lest he should have to pay for a taxi, and often he would wait needlessly for up to an hour so as to avoid making any such foolhardy payment. (Another more ebullient millionaire, Nubar Gulbenkian, saved on taxi fares by purchasing a cab as his personal transport, suitably transformed by a London coachbuilder and complete with chauffeur disguised as a cabbie.) Visitors to Getty's Sussex home, Sutton Place, were surprised to find a pay telephone box installed lest the billionaire's house guests should extravagantly call London. Nor was his day-to-day charitable record any better. Once when an exceedingly distinguished academic made an appeal to him for the restoration of an Oxford college, after much hesitation Getty coughed up — £5. The college returned it.

Another contemporary billionaire is what is tactfully called "careful" with his billions — Daniel K. Ludwig (qv). His strict observance of the maxim "Look after the pennies and the pounds will look after themselves" has led him to enjoy a less than openhanded reputation. To look after the pennies the octogenarian billionaire still walks to his office each morning, owns only an aged car, travels tourist class — a habit he shares with Bunker Hunt — and never smokes or drinks. Once he nearly fired one of his tanker captains for having the temerity to use a paper clip on a two-page report. The enclosing envelope was all that was required, he raged.

A famous miser, John Camden Neild, chose a different course. The son of a prosperous goldsmith, Neild inherited a quarter of a million pounds (£3,986,486 today) from his father when he died in 1814. Thereafter the young man devoted himself single-mindedly to increasing his fortune. He dressed in rags and refused even to have them brushed lest the nap should be damaged. He declined to have an overcoat and refused to undertake even the simplest repairs for the houses of the tenants on his vast estates in Buckinghamshire. To his considerable fury, however, he could not escape his duty as squire to repair the church on his estates at North Marston, but he hit on a way of filling the letter of his obligation, rather than its spirit: he had the tower mended with calico. Which proved less than effective when it began to rain.

When this most unpopular of landlords died it was found that he had left everything he owned to Queen Victoria. The monarch surveyed the size of the bequest, declared she was amused — and accepted.

Not all "golden meanies" are ungenerous only with money. Some are equally careful with time. A notable example of this aberration is the pater familias of the Hunt clan of Dallas, Texas (qv), Haroldson Lafayette Hunt, the son of a Confederate soldier who succeeded in piling up a stash of two billion dollars, partly on a foundation of poker winnings. When asked why he had given up smoking cigars, something which had manifestly given him great pleasure, he replied, "I figured that I wasted $300,000 a year just in the time I spent taking the wrappings off my cigars and lighting them."

It Pays to Advertise

At the beginning of this century retailers began to grasp what could be achieved by advertising — a development that made a number of people suddenly and gratifyingly rich. A few of them managed to combine value with entertainment to such good effect that they became legends in their own time.

Gordon Selfridge, whose Oxford Street store still bears his name, opened it so close to the limits of his credit that it was said he would go bankrupt unless he sold all his stock within the day. An American, Selfridge accordingly resorted to the distinctly un-British expedient of advertising. So delighted was he when the public flocked to buy that he set about capping his store with a giant tower like an obelisk — a pardonable flourish in somebody whose other obsession in life was the Dolly Sisters. It then occurred to him that it would make sense to have his own special tube station, called "Selfridge," but the London Transport Board's attitude about this was unsporting and they refused him permission. Selfridge had to fall back on unilateral action and put his own men to work on extending his do-it-yourself department in the basement in the direction of Bond Street tube station. Sears Holdings, the current owners of the emporium, assure us that work is no longer in progress.

The grocers of the day soon thought equally big and the swashbuckling Sir Thomas Lipton promoted tea as though it was the rarest elixir known to man — and became a millionaire. In his effort to live down the undeniable fact that he was in "trade," Lipton took to ocean racing and challenged repeatedly for the Americas' Cup. In the event he displayed more sportsmanship than success — though his yachts, all christened *Shamrock*, became bywords in England and Tommy Lipton a national hero. Lipton thus became the father of the sponsored sporting event — and sold oceans of tea.

The beginning of the century saw a craze for patent medicines — all fueled with newfangled advertising. Holloway the Pill King made his mark very literally when he had his slogan — "Take Holloway's Pink Pills" — splashed in indelible paint on the sides of the pyramids. The fortune thus generated went into building the Royal Holloway College, a three-times scaled-up red brick replica of a Loire château *(vaut le détour)* on the bosky banks of the Thames at Egham.

Not to be outdone, the French car-czar Citroën hired an airplane to spell out his name in white smoke above the Paris Exposition of 1922, while a fleet of Citroën cars gave grateful citizens lifts to the fair. His fellow countrymen were annoyed and accused him of modeling himself on that vulgar American Henry Ford, to the detriment of the sacred Gallic way of life. Stimulated by their outrage, as well as by his soaring sales, Citroën decided that quickly dispersed advertisements in the air above the Eiffel Tower were not enough and turned his attention to the tower itself. On July 4, 1925, the world was suddenly dazzled by his name shining forth from that landmark, its letters composed of no less than 25,000 electric bulbs.

Rich though Citroën became as a result of all this, it didn't do him much good. The Dolly Sisters (qv) got him too in the end, and like many lesser men before him he finished up flat broke.

Citroën, Lipton, Selfridge and the great American retailers like Bloomingdale: did any of them spare a thought for a predecessor who set an early example of how to become a self-made millionaire as a result of advertising? This was Richard Arkwright, the inventor of the water frame and the spinning jenny. His first success came in hairdressing, entirely as a result of inspired promotion. With a confidence Vidal Sassoon would envy, he had gone into the mane trade in his native Preston, in Lancashire. Unfortunately the only shop he could afford was a dank and smelly back-street basement. A lesser spirit might have quailed, but not so Arkwright. He cut his price by half, to one penny, and erected outside his shop a giant signboard — the first to appear in Preston — with the message: COME TO THE SUBTER-

RANEAN BARBER — HE SHAVES FOR A PENNY. The unkempt citizens of Preston came in droves, the opposition was driven out of business . . . but finally so was Arkwright. To use the parlance of the Harvard Business School, his margins had been shaved too close. He left town to start up again, as an inventor.

That's the trouble with easy-come fortunes . . . they do tend to be easy-go as well. Look at the Englishman John Bloom, who did so much to enliven the sixties by advertising cheap washing machines with an extraordinary array of free bonuses, notably holidays-for-two at inaccessible and unalluring communist beach resorts. Delighted at the prospect of browning their skins as well as whitening their clothes, the public responded and made him a millionaire in months. But then that sleeping giant of the appliance world, Hoover, decided that enough was enough and set about undercutting his prices. Within months Bloom's Black Sea Bubble had burst.

C hip Off the Old Block

There have been a number of references to Texas and Texan millionaires in this book. For addicts of *Dallas* fearful of their soap opera running out of material there is reassurance at hand. While Bunker, Lamar, and William Herbert Hunt were busying themselves with their gas, oil and silver interests, Bunker's eighteen-year-old son, Houston, made $7 million dealing in futures on the pay phone at his college dormitory.

You Should Be in Pictures

There is one billionaire who everybody thinks they know intimately. Trouble is, we all get his name wrong, confusing him hopelessly with the fictional character based on him. The fictional billionaire: Orson Welles's Citizen Kane, newspaper magnate. The real-life character: William Randolph Hearst, newspaper magnate.

In truth, so close are the characters that it's almost impossible to separate them—although nobody has suggested that Hearst had a sled—or anything else for that matter—named Rosebud. Much of the rest, however, is true: and truth, as Hearst himself would have said, is stranger than fiction.

Even if he had no sled, at ten years old the infant Willie Hearst did get around to asking his mother: "When I grow up, Mamma, can I live in Windsor Castle?" And when Mamma said, "No, dear," came back with: "Then will you buy me the Louvre?"

The Louvre being temporarily unavailable, Hearst set about converting the paltry eight million dollars ($30,400,000 today) his father had left him into a vast newspaper empire and finally built himself something on the same lines. Incidentally, on the way, Hearst had fallen for the beautiful but glacial movie star Marion Davies, for whom he bought the odd Hollywood studio.

His first shot at finding the home of his dreams was an eleventh century castle in Wales, but he quickly moved on to an estate near San Francisco called Wintoon—Marion

dubbed it "spitoon"—where he erected a Bavarian village, complete with timbered chalets, among which the happy couple wandered in lederhosen and Tyrolean hats.

However, Hearst must have shared some of Marion's distaste for the place since he then moved on to the fabled San Simeon—the Xanadu of *Citizen Kane*—where in some 200,000 acres between Los Angeles and San Francisco he built the most fabulous palace of the New World, mostly out of bits and pieces of palaces of the Old World.

On one occasion he bought a Spanish Cistercian monastery, sight unseen, to say nothing of Charles the First's bed, in which he and the lovely Marion disported themselves. Statues, armor, and entire castles, schlosses and châteaus were brought in numbered packing cases from Europe—and never unpacked nor reassembled. In all, Hearst spent $50 million ($190,000,000 today) on art treasures, until finally he ran out of money and had to sell most of his hoard. Not that he seemed bothered by it, proclaiming as he did: "Pleasure is what you can afford to pay for it. . . ."

*O*nce Bitten

One balmy evening in Rio de Janeiro the Count de Riboissier, who was on a visit to the city, went out to take the air.
After a leisurely stroll he decided to return by tram and
during the ride had the gallantry to rise from his seat in
order to offer it to a lady. Alas, the good count missed his
footing on the slippery floor of the swaying public con-
veyance and broke his leg in several places. Having no
money on him and being unable to explain who he was to
the concerned crowd that soon collected, he ended in the
nearest charity hospital.

His leg recovered, but his nervous system did not. "You
cannot conceive," he told his friends after his release,
"what such a pesthouse is like. From now on I shall travel
fully equipped for any emergency!"

Accordingly, from that day on Count de Riboissier always
traveled with a thousand dollars' worth of each of the following currencies in his pockets: pounds sterling, francs,
guldens, zlotys, milreis, taler, yen, pesos, marks, pengö and
drachmas — in all, some ten thousand dollars ($56,000 to-
day).

Now, if only he had carried a gold American Express
card . . .

*A*fter the Ball...

Most of the rich have liked partying, and since the less rich like being the admiring guests of their financial betters, there is a never-ending stream of party fodder. Though perhaps not always with the happiest of results — as the slightly down-market guests of the Emperor Heliogabalus discovered when one of them remarked how pleasant it would be to be smothered in the scent of roses that adorned the imperial table, and the rest agreed. Taking them at their word, the next time the same guests came to dinner the emperor had several tons of petals dumped over the dinner table. The guests' reaction on this occasion passed unrecorded. They had suffocated.

Dining with royalty has often proved dangerous, even — or maybe especially — in the privacy of one's own home. The millionaire Cardinal Wolsey, for instance, asked Henry VIII to lunch at his newly completed house at Hampton Court — only to have his monarch purloin the whole place.

Another party for a monarch that ended in tears was held in 1661 by Nicolas Fouquet, Louis XIV of France's hyper-rich finance minister. Fouquet had just completed a magnificent château at Vaux-le-Vicomte when he invited his royal employer to a housewarming party. Louis wined and dined, then duly admired the fifty ornamental fountains bubbling with wine in the gardens, and in the evening enjoyed the premiere of a play by Molière. Next morning he had his host arrested for embezzlement. The one-time millionaire died in prison on March 23, 1680. The party, on this occasion at least, was well and truly over.

No fatal consequences, however, were recorded during the endless whirl of parties that illuminated the world of the transatlantic super-rich at the end of the nineteenth century. One enormously rich clan vied with another until the whole of New York and Long Island seemed to be having a gigantic hoedown. Most formidable — and first in — were the railroad-rich Vanderbilts; a Mrs. Alva Vanderbilt set the family fashion, building an all-white marble palace specially for party-giving. The building, no doubt in deference to the almost imperial importance of the family, was based on the Temple of the Sun at Baalbek. To launch it Mrs. Alva held a fancy-dress ball that cost more than a quarter of a million dollars. Then, tired of the restrictions of the Marble Palace, Mrs. Vanderbilt ran up a proper schloss — "Vanderbilt Palace" — at 640 Fifth Avenue. Here, in order to make party-giving even more agreeable, a copy of the ballroom at Versailles was built — the fruits of the labor of six hundred all-American builders and two hundred and fifty craftsmen.

No party, however, had quite the éclat of the Bradley-Martin ball. Indeed, so amazing were the proceedings that in time they came to be immortalized in a musical by no less an artist than Oscar Hammerstein. This once-famous bash took place in New York in February 1897. The hitherto unknown out-of-town host and hostess had let it be known that theirs was to be the ball of this or any other season. The trouble was that the outside world took some exception to the extraordinary publicity that surrounded the Bradley-Martins' dream of extravagance — in this case a $200,000 costume ball with each guest attired as a historical figure. Pulpits around America thundered against the Bradley-Martins, who remained more or less calm in spite of the threats of hell-fire that rained down on them from every side. Mrs. Bradley-Martin, indeed, went so far as to issue a statement claiming that, far from being a senseless extravagance, her ball was rather a selfless plan to ameliorate the lot of the working classes by providing work for teams of otherwise unemployed hairdressers, milliners and florists.

Controversy raged, but the hosts had made an ingenious point. Numerous artisans and tradesmen *were* kept in gainful employ, in part by providing some six thousand mauve orchids for the corsages of the Bradley-Martin guests. Additionally, some four hundred carriages waited outside the site of the party in order to take the guests home after they had eaten and drunk their substantial fill, pausing only from time to time to admire their hostess's gown, on which sparkled some $200,000 ($1,120,000 today) worth of diamonds. One hack estimated the guests used up among them five hundred pounds of rouge, two and a half barrels of flour and enough powder puffs to make up a pile ten feet by six feet wide — doubtless all the work of disadvantaged artisans.

Unfortunately for the gracious hosts, the tax authorities, although not among the guests, were among the millions who had followed the controversy surrounding the "ball of the year" with close attention. Perhaps, since tax men are undoubtedly "trade" in the eyes of any self-respecting hostess, they simply thought that Mrs. Bradley-Martin's protestations that she was merely providing employment for the laboring classes applied also to revenue men. Whatever their reasoning, they doubled the Bradley-Martins' tax assessment the next year. In disgust the couple upped and left America for Europe forever.

Considering such flights of extravagance and the general diminution of fortunes in Europe owing to the growth of another iniquitous invention of the tax authorities — namely, income tax — it is hardly surprising that party-giving rather somewhat declined in most European countries after the Great War. Not that the rich didn't do the best they could, employing such devices as hiring Elsa Maxwell to throw mammoth shindigs for them. But somehow it wasn't the same anymore.

But, with the birth of great new wealth in the east, help was at hand. In October 1971, the shah of Iran, Light of the Aryans, decided to fete the 2,500th anniversary of the Persian Empire. In spite of the fact that he himself was the son of a mutinous though strong-minded sergeant who had staged a coup d'etat less than fifty years before, the shah decided to hold the party to end all parties to celebrate the continuity of the dynastic tradition. His beautiful wife wore a crown from Van Cleef and Arpels — and at the end of the proceedings the shah addressed the tomb of Darius the Great through a megaphone.

It was the party itself, however, that lingers in the memory of the super-rich. The guests found themselves lodged in a special cloth-of-gold tented village in Persepolis (rather like the Field of the Cloth of Gold of glorious memory, some four hundred years earlier). They numbered five hundred and included nine kings, five queens, sixteen presidents and two sultans — as well as assorted millionaires. The tents were decorated by Jansen of Paris, complete with crystal by Baccarat, porcelain from Limoges, damask linens, Persian carpets and one luxury denied Darius — air-conditioning. Maxim's of Paris sent over one hundred and fifty chefs to carve up among them 7,700 pounds of meat and 8,000 pounds of butter and to ladle out 1,000 pints of cream. Twenty-five thousand bottles of wine, selected by the sommelier, were sent out to Persepolis a month early so they could settle before they were emptied down the throats of the world's super-rich in the arid desert. The menu consisted of partridge with fois gras and truffle stuffing, followed by filets of sole stuffed with caviar. (This combination did not appeal to everyone — Sultan Qaboos of Oman requested, and got, caviar and kebab.) For those who remained peckish there were ample supplies of quails eggs and other trifles; while the chefs from Maxim's maintained round-the-clock tent service.

Back in Tehran one of the guests was kindly loaned the shah's personal chauffeur by his host. When they took a wrong turning it became necessary to reverse. Shamefacedly the chauffeur admitted he did not know how — as the shah's driver he had never had to.

Money Hath Charms

As I walk along the Bois de Boulong
With an independent air
You can hear the girls declare
He must be a millionaire
You can hear them sigh and wish to die
You can see them wink the other eye
At the man who broke the bank at Monte Carlo

FRED GILBERT

One of the fabled delights of being a millionaire is the enhanced opportunity to serenade beautiful women. Take, for
example, Senhor Jorginho Guinle. In the course of a few
years' effort, representing the Brazilian government in Hollywood from 1940 onward, he squired, as they say, all of the
following dames: Veronica Lake, Lana Turner, Rita Hay-
worth, Susan Hayward, Hedy Lamarr, Jayne Mansfield,
Anita Ekberg, Romy Schneider, Zsa Zsa Gabor, Kim Novak
and Norma Jean Baker a.k.a. Marilyn Monroe. And all this
on coffee. Senhor Guinle is still alive and well and living in
Rio, with a girl of twenty-three.

By Their Dress Shall Ye Know Them

In the past, millionaires — or most of them, at least — liked not only to live it up generally, but also to show even the most casual passer-by how very rich they were. It is only recently that ostentation has begun to be unfashionable. It was certainly de rigueur in the days of our first example of dressing rich: Henry Percy, Fifth Earl of Northumberland, a distant millionaire heavy with the dust of history, though not — one can be sure — with the dust of sartorial neglect.

We can speak with such confidence because Henry, who lived in all but royal state during the sixteenth century, is known to have employed a hundred and sixteen persons simply as his body servants. He made provision for fifty-seven visitors at his table every day, regardless of who (if anybody) was expected (did he perhaps serve an equal number of varieties of food? H. J. Heinz should be told). But above all His Grace had a thing about clothes. It was not only he himself who must outshine his neighbors, it was everyone in his retinue as well. When he sent his private army to fight the French outside Calais, he provided each individual soldier in that army with the following wardrobe:

1   20 pairs of hose
2   25 pairs of boots
3   21 pairs of garters
4   14 hats and a bonnet
5   1 fur-lined night gown
6   16 scarlet night bonnets
7   Several complete suits of armor

The troops were happy, and — for those uncertain times — remarkably free from the tendency to mutiny. The Earl of Northumberland, however, bankrupted himself and almost ended his life in jail for debt.

No doubt, had he but been able to know him, the earl would have felt a certain affinity with another member of the House of Lords — namely Alfred Lord Rothschild who flourished some three hundred years later. In the petty cash book for the year 1890 in the bank's New Court offices is the following item, double entered in blue-black ink in a copperplate hand: "Bought for Alfred Rothschild — one mink footwarmer."

No doubt the sixteenth century earl, shivering in the draughty keep at Alnwick Castle, would have had one if he could.

Similar "dressing up to kill" took place on the other side of the Atlantic too. The American version of Beau Brummell was a swell who rejoiced in the name of O. C. McIntyre. His preferred shop was Sulka, from which he would buy twelve-dollar silk ties by the hundred. However, he is best remembered there for having ordering on one occasion no less than fifty brocaded, satin-faced, silk-corded smoking jackets and dressing gowns.

However, no self-seeking millionaire in America in the thirties would consider having his clothes made anywhere but in London. Then as now, such men would seek out a reliable firm, who extended the proper courtesies and credit. Prominent among these, for many years, has been the Savile Row company of Henry Poole and Co.

One of their cash customers was the American millionaire Berry Wall, who had Poole's run him up some five hundred complete outfits. It was the bare minimum he could do with, since Mr. Wall would change his clothes at least six times a day — which must have occasioned an investment of some fifty thousand dollars ($360,000 today). His laundry bills are, alas, unavailable.

Another millionaire who prided herself on having a costume fit for every occasion was Mrs. J. J. Brown — but her wardrobe was tested to the utmost when the lady ran foul of an iceberg. For the intrepid Mrs. Brown was a passenger on the *Titanic*. Fortunately she had the foresight to pack a copious wardrobe, including several large pairs of walking bloomers and numerous sets of long johns, as well as assorted scarves, muffs and so forth. From among her vast collection of furs, Mrs. Brown had after much thought decided to pack a four thousand dollar ($22,400 today) Russian sable muff in which she habitually concealed a silver Colt .45 revolver, as well as her world-famous sixty-thousand-dollar ($336,000 today) chinchilla evening cape.

She must have expected the voyage to be cold, and as it turned out it was. Mrs. J. J. Brown was to spend many hours tossing around in a succession of small boats, in the company of survivors who inexplicably seemed to have been selected by the Almighty with little or no consideration for their social position or wealth. Mrs. Brown was to remark on this in retrospect, but at the time she decided to overlook it and set about distributing her clothing little by little to those less fortunate than herself. The first garments of which she divested herself were her woolen underwear. Other less intimate garments were passed out later, while the robust millionairess kept for herself only the minimum that decency and warmth required.

To encourage those whose enthusiasm still flagged in spite of this heart- and body-warming generosity, Mrs. J. J. Brown then drew her Colt revolver from the depths of the sable muff and fired it into the threatening waves that surrounded them. Not surprisingly, she so galvanized the entire group of shipwrecked passengers in her lifeboat that they all survived.

Not Everything Comes to Him...

One day, late in 1949, Jack J. Wurm, an unemployed waiter of San Francisco, California, was walking disconsolately down the beach at dawn, and found a bottle bobbing up and down in the tide. From the bottle he extracted a letter—which proved to be the last will and testament of Margaret "Daisy" Alexander, the billionaire daughter of the sewing machine tycoon Isaac Singer. The will read: "I leave my entire estate to the lucky person who finds this bottle and to my attorney, Barry Cohan, half and half."

The bottle had been traveling the seas for ten years, having been cast into the waters off Beachy Head by the eccentric millionairess, shortly before her death in 1939. Urgent inquiries showed that Mr. Wurm and the presumably less disadvantaged Mr. Cohan stood to split some twelve million dollars and an income of $160,000. Mr. Wurm was over the moon. There was only one problem. The will was not witnessed—and the Singer Company declined to pay.

Keeping Your Head Down

Some millionaires have taken their passion for privacy to the point of mania, not only by retiring to islands or behind high walls, but also by resorting to an unlovely assortment of savage dogs and heavily armed guards. Others develop a sort of paranoia about becoming well enough known to be recognized by their fellow citizens — maybe through fear of kidnapping, maybe through a natural and lovely shyness.

Harry Hyams is one such. He is a property developer who became famous in the 1960s for building "Centre Point," a skyscraper in Central London, and then working out that there was more money to be made by keeping it empty than by filling it with paying tenants. (This extraordinary phenomenon is due to the fact that empty office buildings go up in value quicker than occupied ones — and no taxes are due until somebody moves in.) Anyway, Mr. Hyams has always had such a horror of being photographed that no Fleet Street paper ever had his mug shot on file. An especially enterprising free-lance lensman even went to the length of secreting himself by the polling booth during a General Election day, sure that he would capture a shot of the shy billionaire. He succeeded in recording for posterity all the inhabitants of Harry Hyams's home village, but that year the millionaire decided not to visit the polling booth.

More extreme in their desire for privacy were Homer Collyer and his brother Langley, who lived in amazing squalor in a decaying house in what had once been a fashionable section of Harlem. The brothers holed up there after their mother, to whom they were extravagantly devoted, separated from their father, whom they equally extravagantly detested, one hot night in 1909. Homer was an Admiralty lawyer, while his brother Langley was an engineer and concert pianist. When their mother died in 1929 they both gave up their jobs and became recluses, even to the extent of allowing the water and light to be cut off rather than admit a stranger into the house. Homer went blind shortly after his mother died and never went out again — while his brother Langley fed him one hundred oranges a day in the vain hope of restoring his sight. When not peeling oranges Langley was hyperactive — carrying cans of water from the park — a necessity once the water had been cut off — and scavenging the streets at night. But above all, he spent his time building elaborate booby traps and barricading doors and windows with piles of debris and rubble. Though the neighbors watched fascinated, nobody knew how and where Langley Collyer got in and out of his house.

Then one day in March 1947, alerted by dreadful odors emanating from the first floor of the barricaded house, the police broke in to find the decomposing body of blind and paralyzed Homer Collyer — dead of starvation. A crowd gathered at once in the hope of at least glimpsing the fabled treasure of the Collyers, a hoard that generations of neighborhood gossip had increased in size till it rivaled in popular imagination all the gold of El Dorado. In fact, all that was uncovered was a maze of rubble through which Langley had burrowed little tunnels like a rat.

Working from the basement up, the City of New York Refuse Service removed a hundred and twenty tons of rubble — including fourteen grand pianos upon which

Langley had presumably once played; the chassis of a model T Ford; hundreds of discarded toys and clothes, and a mountain of unopened mail. The bulk of the Collyer brothers' possessions, however, consisted of hundreds of unread newspapers, neatly piled and folded. Langley had been keeping them for Homer to read once the one hundred daily oranges had restored his sight.

At first it seemed that there was no sign of Langley to be found, but finally, burrowing his way through yet another newspaper tunnel, a fireman came upon his body. He had been crushed to death by one of his own booby traps — and then savagely gnawed by rats. In thirty-four bank books — all the searchers could uncover among the thousands of sheets of paper of all sizes — were deposited some $100,000. Much of the brothers' other wealth, according to popular legend, was never found.

But the prince of reclusive and secretive millionaires, as well as the prince of all tunnelers, must have been the vastly rich Fifth Duke of Portland. In his huge house at Welbeck he occupied only three rooms — with two letter-boxes cut into the outside doors, one for incoming and one for outgoing letters. His Grace thus avoided having to talk even to his own servants.

But above all, he took to tunnels, as some aristocrats have taken to paintings and some to women. The first tunnel that His Grace built ran from his home at Welbeck to Work-sop railway station, so that he could travel from one to the other unobserved. His incognito was further defended by the use of a small wagonette with drawn blinds that traveled on a narrow-gauge track through the tunnel, His Grace huddled up on board. Emerging from the Portland private tunnel, the wagonette was then loaded, still shrouded, onto the London train.

After this happy experience with tunnels, the molelike duke took to excavation in a big way. Soon the earth below his broad acres was riddled with tunnels through which he could pass in inky darkness and enveloping obscurity. Gangs of men were employed on these subterranean follies — and sometimes His Grace had literally thousands of navvies on his pay roll. No doubt he had taken seriously the admonition that it is "the duty of the wealthy man to give employment to the artisan," since little or no other purpose could have accounted for His Grace's mania. On one single occasion he spent £113,000 on iron and steel girders for one particular project — a particularly daunting scheme in which the mere joy of a tunnel had given way in the duke's fancy to the construction at Welbeck of an underground library and ballroom. To negate as far as possible the chills and damp inherent in living underground, His Grace had gas and electricity connected in his diggings. A thoughtful employer at all times, the tunneling duke provided his subterranean work force with umbrellas to keep their heads dry and donkeys upon which to ride through the underground mazes, thus keeping their feet dry. And above ground, for the diversion of his navvies and their families, His Grace built one of the first roller-skating rinks in England. His successors, however, faced with subsidence and flooding in the most improbable parts of the estate, found the eccentricities of their ancestor rather less endearing than did the outside world.

But all such tales of reclusive billionaires pale into insignificance next to the familiar story of Howard Hughes, a billionaire who, at the age of eighteen, parlayed his share in an oil drill bit company into an aviation, gambling and film business fortune of fabulous proportions.

In 1952, after a series of lawsuits, Hughes went into total seclusion, buying much of Las Vegas, the better to preserve his privacy in the most anonymous town in the United States. Here, surrounded by Mormon bodyguards, his feet clad in Kleenex boxes to ward off an imagined plague of germs, Hughes went invisibly but firmly mad. He finally expired of malnutrition and neglect in a chartered Lear jet aircraft on April 5, 1976. According to popular legend he had cut neither his nails nor his hair for a decade. He left one and a half billion dollars, but no will. In the words of Ted Morgan: "Howard Hughes was able to afford the luxury of madness, like a man who not only thinks he's Napoleon, but hires an army to prove it."

*E*pilogue

"Money is a singular thing. It ranks with love as man's greatest source of joy. And with death as his greatest source of anxiety. It differs from an automobile, a mistress or cancer, in being equally important to those who have it, and those who do not."—John Kenneth Galbraith.

Galbraith was certainly right about almost everybody's consuming interest in money and the strength of their feelings about it. But once you try to define those feelings, the chance of any agreement rapidly diminishes. The happiness quotient is a case in point. Back in 1933 Ogden Nash wrote, "Certainly there are lots of things in life that money won't buy, but it's funny—have you ever tried to buy them without money?" On the other hand John Lennon and Paul McCartney, millionaires already, wrote, "I don't care too much for money, for money can't buy me love."

The compilers would like to have found a simple, sure-fire recipe for instant enrichment to pass on as a gift to their readers. This they have not managed to achieve. The best they can do is to transmit the advice of Oliver Wendell Holmes: "Put not your trust in money, but put your money in trust." And the words of Larry Niven who, when he was asked, "What is the best advice you have ever been given?" replied, "On my twenty-first birthday my father said, 'Son, here's a million dollars. Don't lose it.'" Kin Hubbard's recipe was also a simple one: "The safest way to double your money is to fold it over once and put it in your pocket." (Mr. Hubbard was clearly someone who knew the whole sub-

ject pretty well. He also said on one occasion, "When a fellow says it isn't the money but the principle of the thing, it's the money.")

But maybe we should not take this lack of a Midas formula too much to heart. After all, even King Midas himself, the patron saint of millionaires if ever there was one, found that turning everything he touched to gold, even his food and his wine, was a decidedly mixed blessing.

So, knowing only too well what Saki meant when he said, "I am living so far beyond my income that we may almost be said to be living apart," the compilers can only suggest that the advice given by Artemus Ward should be pondered: "Let us all be happy and live within our means. Even if we have to borrow the money to do it with."